T0208594

IN DEFENCE
OF THE TERROR

IN DEFENCE
OF THE TERROR

Liberty or Death in the French Revolution

SOPHIE WAHNICH

Translated by David Fernbach

With a Foreword by Slavoj Žižek

VERSO

London • New York

Liberté • Égalité • Fraternité

RÉPUBLIQUE FRANÇAISE

This book is supported by the Institut français as part of the Burgess programme (www.frenchbooknews.com)

This paperback edition published by Verso 2015
First published in English by Verso 2012
© Verso 2012
Translation © David Fernbach 2012, 2015
First published as *La liberté ou la mort: Essai sur la Terreur et le terrorisme*
© La Fabrique éditions 2003
Introduction © Slavoj Žižek 2012, 2015

All rights reserved

The moral rights of the authors have been asserted

1 3 5 7 9 10 8 6 4 2

Verso

UK: 6 Meard Street, London W1F 0EG
US: 388 Atlantic Ave, Brooklyn, NY 11217

www.versobooks.com

Verso is the imprint of New Left Books

ISBN- 13: 978-1-78478-202-3
eISBN-13: 978-1-84467-933-1 (US)
eISBN-13: 978-1-78168-399-6 (UK)

British Library Cataloguing in Publication Data
A catalogue record for this book is available from the British Library

The Library of Congress Has Cataloged the Hardcover Edition as Follows:

Wahnich, Sophie.
[Liberté ou la mort. English.]
In defence of the terror : liberty or death in the French Revolution / Sophie Wahnich ; translated by David Fernbach ; with a foreword by Slavojіiiek.
p. cm.
Original publication: Paris : La Fabrique Éditions, c2003: La liberté ou la mort.
Includes bibliographical references.
ISBN 978-1-84467-862-4 (hardback)—ISBN 978-1-84467-933-1 (ebook)
1. France—History—Reign of Terror, 1793–1794. 2. France—History—Revolution, 1789–1799. 3. France—Politics and government—1789–1799. 4. Terrorism. I. Title.
DC176.5.W3413 2012
944.04'4—dc23
2012013023

Typeset in Sabon by Hewer Text UK Ltd, Edinburgh
Printed in the United States

For Lorenzo and Julia

CONTENTS

I want never to forget how I was forced to become – for how long? – a monster of justice and intolerance, a narrow-minded simplifier, an arctic character uninterested in anyone who was not in league with him to kill the dogs of hell.

– René Char[1]

1 René Char, 'Recherche de la base et du sommet. Billets à Francis Curel, II' (1943), *Œuvres complètes*, Paris: Gallimard, 1983, p. 633.

FOREWORD: THE DARK MATTER OF VIOLENCE, OR, PUTTING TERROR IN PERSPECTIVE

Slavoj Žižek

From time to time, a book appears about which we can say: we were not waiting *merely* for a book like this; this is *the* book we were waiting for. Sophie Wahnich's *In Defence of the Terror* is such a rare book: it cuts into the very heart of today's ethico-political predicament. How can a book about the French Revolution do this?

When, in 1953, Zhou En Lai, the Chinese premier, was in Geneva for the peace negotiations to end the Korean war, a French journalist asked him what he thought about the French Revolution; Chou replied: 'It is still too early to tell.' The events of 1990 proved him spectacularly right: with the disintegration of the 'people's democracies', the struggle for the historical place of the French Revolution flared up again. The liberal revisionists tried to impose the notion that the demise of communism in 1989 occurred at exactly the right moment: it marked the end of the era which began in 1789, the final failure of the statist-revolutionary model which first entered the scene with the Jacobins.

Nowhere is the dictum 'every history is a history of the present' more true than in the case of the French Revolution: its historiographical reception has always closely mirrored the twists and turns of later political

struggles. The identifying mark of all kinds of conserv-
atives is a predictably flat rejection: the French
Revolution was a catastrophe from its very beginning.
The product of the godless modern mind, it is at the
same time to be interpreted as God's judgement on
humanity's wicked ways – so its traces should of course
be kicked over as thoroughly as possible. The typical
liberal attitude is a more differentiated one: its formula
is '1789 without 1793'. In short, what the sensitive liberals want is a decaffeinated revolution, a revolution
which does not smell of a revolution. François Furet
proposed another liberal approach: he tried to deprive
the French Revolution of its status as the founding
event of modern democracy, relegating it to a historical
anomaly. In short, Furet's aim was to de-eventalize the
French Revolution: it is no longer (as for a tradition
stemming from Kant and Hegel) the defining moment
of modernity, but a local accident with no global significance, one conditioned by the specifically French
tradition of absolute monarchy. Jacobin state central-
ism is only possible, then, against the background of
the 'L'état c'est moi' of Louis XIV. There was a historical necessity to assert the modern principles of
personal freedom, etc., but – as the English example
demonstrates – the same could have been much more
effectively achieved in a more peaceful way . . .
Radicals are, on the contrary, possessed by what Alain
Badiou called the 'passion of the Real': if you say A –
equality, human rights and freedoms – then you should
not shirk its consequences but instead gather the courage to say B – the terror needed to really defend and
assert A.

Both liberal and conservative critics of the French
Revolution present it as a founding event of modern
'totalitarianism': the taproot of all the worst evils of
the twentieth century – the Holocaust, the Gulag, up
to the 9/11 attacks – is to be sought in the Jacobin
'Reign of Terror'. The perpetrators of Jacobin crimes

are either denounced as bloodthirsty monsters, or, in a more nuanced approach, one admits that they were personally honest and pure, but then adds that this very feature made their fanaticism all the more dangerous. The conclusion is thus the well-known cynical wisdom: better corruption than ethical purity, better a direct lust for power than obsession with one's mission.[1]

Wahnich's book systematically undermines this predominant *doxa*. In a detailed historical analysis of the stages of Jacobin Terror, she first demonstrates how this Terror was not an uncontrolled explosion of destructive madness, but a precisely planned and controlled attempt to prevent such an explosion. She does what Furet wanted to do, but from an opposite perspective: instead of denouncing Terror as an outburst of some eternal 'totalitarian' which explodes from time to time (millenarian peasants' revolts, twentieth-century communist revolutions . . .), Wahnich provides its historical context, resuscitating all the dramatic tenor of the revolutionary process. And then, in a detailed comparison between the French revolutionary Terror and recent fundamentalist terrorism, she renders visible their radical discontinuity, especially the gap that separates their underlying notions of justice. The first step towards correct politics is to break with false symmetries and similarities.

However, what is much more interesting is that, beneath all these diverging opinions, there seems to be a shared perception that 1989 marks the end of the epoch

---

1   Recall how, decades ago, Jeanne Kirkpatrick, one of the US foreign policy ideologists, drew a distinction between Rightist authoritarianism and Leftist totalitarianism, privileging the first: precisely because Rightist authoritarian leaders care only about their power and wealth, they are much less dangerous than the fanatical Leftists who are ready to risk their lives for their cause. Is this distinction not at work today, in the way the US privileges a corrupt authoritarianism in Saudi Arabia over Iran's fundamentalism?

which began in 1789 – the end of a certain 'paradigm', as we like to put it today: the paradigm of a revolutionary process that is focused on taking over state power and then using this power as a lever to accomplish global social transformation. Even the 'postmodern' Left (from Antonio Negri to John Holloway) emphasizes that a new revolution should break with this fetishization of state power as the ultimate prize and focus on the much deeper 'molecular' level of transforming daily practices. It is at this critical point that Wahnich's book intervenes: its underlying premise is that this shift to 'molecular' activities outside the scope of state power is in itself a symptom of the Left's crisis, an indication that today's Left (in the developed countries) is not ready to confront the topic of violence in all its ambiguity – a topic which is usually obfuscated by the fetish of 'Terror'. This ambiguity was clearly described more than a century ago by Mark Twain, who wrote apropos of the French Revolution in *A Connecticut Yankee in King Arthur's Court*:

> There were two 'Reigns of Terror' if we would but remember it and consider it; the one wrought murder in hot passion, the other in heartless cold blood; the one lasted mere months, the other had lasted a thousand years; . . . our shudders are all for the 'horrors' of the minor Terror, the momentary Terror, so to speak; whereas, what is the horror of swift death by the axe, compared with life-long death from hunger, cold, insult, cruelty, and heart-break? . . . A city cemetery could contain the coffins filled by that brief Terror which we have all been so diligently taught to shiver at and mourn over; but all France could hardly contain the coffins filled by that older and real Terror – that unspeakably bitter and awful Terror which none of us have been taught to see in its vastness or pity as it deserves.[2]

---

2   Mark Twain, *A Connecticut Yankee in King Arthur's Court*, New York: Random House, 2001, p. 114.

Does not the same duality characterize our present? At the forefront of our minds these days, 'violence' signals acts of crime and terror, let alone great wars. One should learn to step back, to disentangle oneself from the fascinating lure of this directly visible 'subjective' violence – violence performed by a clearly identifiable agent. We need to perceive the contours of the background which generates such outbursts. A step back enables us to identify a violence that sustains our very efforts to fight violence and to promote tolerance: the 'objective' violence inscribed into the smooth functioning of our economic and political systems. The catch is that subjective and objective violence cannot be perceived from the same standpoint: subjective violence is experienced as such against the background of a non-violent zero-level of 'civility'. It is seen as a perturbation of the normal, peaceful state of things. However, objective violence is precisely the violence inherent in this 'normal' state of things. Objective violence is invisible since it sustains the very zero-level standard against which we perceive something as being subjective violence. Systemic violence is thus something like the notorious 'dark matter' of physics, the counterpart to an all-too-visible subjective violence. It may be invisible, but it has to be taken into account if one is to make sense of what otherwise seem to be 'irrational' explosions of subjective violence. Let us take a quick look at some of the cases of this invisible violence.

The story of Kathryn Bolkovac,[3] recently made into a film (*The Whistleblower*, dir. Larysa Kondracki, 2010), cannot but terrify any honest observer. In 1998 Bolkovac, a US police officer, successfully applied for a place in the UN's International Police Task Force in Bosnia-Herzegovina – under the auspices of a prominent

---

3   See the review of Bolkovac's book, *The Whistleblower*, in Daisy Sindelar, 'In New Book, Whistle-Blower Alleges US, UN Involvement in Bosnian Sex Trafficking', Radio Free Europe/Radio Liberty, 9 February 2011, at rferl.org.

defence contractor, DynCorp – and upon arrival, was assigned to a task force that targeted violence against women. Still new to this position, Bolkovac began to follow up leads which exposed a local sex-trafficking ring, apparently run by the Serbian mafia and dealing in very young girls from former communist-bloc countries – some of these girls were no older than twelve. But another link quickly surfaced: the girls' johns seemed to include UN contractors in Bosnia, and possibly some of Bolkovac's colleagues. Moreover, there were strong indications that UN personnel colluded with or even helped operate sex-trafficking rings in the region, and saw a profit from it.

Shocked by her findings, Bolkovac filed a series of reports with her superiors, but they were all either shelved or returned to her as 'solved'. Nothing was done, and nothing changed – until Bolkovac was demoted and then sacked for 'gross misconduct', well before her contract was up. Finally warned that her life was in danger, she was reduced to flight and left Bosnia with her investigative files and little else.

Bolkovac proceeded to sue DynCorp for 'wrongful termination', and the suit was decided in her favour. As a result, DynCorp dismissed seven of its contractors in Bosnia for 'unacceptable behavior' and publicized changes to its screening protocols. But this sex-trafficking scandal does not seem to have tarnished the company. DynCorp has continued to net massive State Department contracts, despite accusations of criminal misconduct in places like Afghanistan and Iraq. For example, a US diplomatic cable released by WikiLeaks cites DynCorp personnel who were seen taking drugs and hiring 'dancing boys', a polite name for underage male prostitutes (and DynCorp is in Afghanistan, we should note, to train the new Afghan police corps).

The *New York Times* reviewer granted that '*The Whistleblower* tells a story so repellent that it is almost beyond belief.' However, in an incredible ideological *tour de force*, the same reviewer went on to denounce the film's very truthfulness as the cause of its aesthetic failure: '*The Whistleblower* ultimately fizzles by withholding any cathartic sense that justice was done, or ever will be done, once Kathryn spills the beans to the British news media.'[4] It is true, I suppose, that in real life we are far from the 'cathartic sense' of films like *All the President's Men* or *The Pelican Brief*, in which the final disclosure of political crimes brings a kind of emotional relief and satisfaction . . .

And is not the lesson of Libya after Gaddafi's fall a similar one? Now we have learned that Gaddafi's secret services fully collaborated with their Western counterparts, including participating in programs of rendition. We can perhaps discern this kind of complicity between 'rogue states' and the Western guardians of human rights at its most radical in Congo. The cover story of *Time* magazine on 5 June 2006 was 'The Deadliest War In the World' – a detailed report on how some 4 million people have died in Congo over the last decade as the result of political violence. None of the usual humanitarian uproar followed, just a couple of reader's letters – as if some filtering mechanism blocked this news from achieving its full impact. To put it cynically, *Time* picked the wrong victim in the struggle for hegemony in suffering – it should have stuck to the list of usual suspects: Muslim women and their plight, the oppression in Tibet . . . It is Congo today which has effectively re-emerged as a Conradean 'heart of darkness', yet no one dares to confront it. The death of a West Bank Palestinian child, not to mention an Israeli or an American, is mediatically worth thousands of times more than the death of a nameless Congolese. Why this ignorance?

---

4   See Stephen Holden, 'American in Bosnia Discovers the Horrors of Human Trafficking', *New York Times*, 4 August 2011.

On 30 October 2008, the Associated Press reported that Laurent Nkunda, the rebel general besieging Congo's eastern provincial capital Goma, said that he wanted direct talks with the government about his objections to a billion-dollar deal that gives China access to the country's vast mineral riches in exchange for a railway and highway. As problematic (neocolonialist) as this deal may be, it poses a vital threat to the interests of local warlords, since its eventual success would create the infrastructural base for the Democratic Republic of Congo as a functioning united state.

Back in 2001, a UN investigation on the illegal exploitation of natural resources in Congo found that conflict in the country is mainly about access to and control and trade of five key mineral resources: coltan, diamonds, copper, cobalt and gold. According to this report, the exploitation of Congo's natural resources by local warlords and foreign armies is 'systematic and systemic', and the leaders of Uganda and Rwanda in particular (closely followed by Zimbabwe and Angola) had turned their armed forces into armies of business. The report concludes that permanent civil war and the disintegration of Congo 'has created a "win–win" situation for all belligerents. The only loser in this huge business venture is the Congolese people'. One should bear in mind this good old 'economic-reductionist' background when one reads in the media about primitive ethnic passions exploding yet again in the African 'heart of darkness' . . . Beneath the facade of ethnic warfare, we thus discern the contours of global capitalism.

Today's capitalism likes to present itself as ethically responsible; however, its 'ethical' face is the result of a complex process of ideological abstraction or obliteration. Companies dealing with raw materials extracted and exported in suspicious conditions (using de facto slaves or child labour) effectively practise the art of 'ethical cleansing', the true business counterpart to ethnic cleansing: through reselling, etc., such practices obscure the origins of materials which are produced under conditions unacceptable to our Western societies.

There definitely is a lot of darkness in the dense Congolese jungle – but its heart lies elsewhere, in the bright executive offices of our banks and high-tech companies. In order to truly awaken from the capitalist 'dogmatic dream' (as Kant would have put it) and see this other true heart of darkness, one should re-apply to our situation Brecht's old quip from *The Threepenny Opera*: 'What is the robbing of a bank compared to the founding of a new bank?' What is the stealing of a couple of thousand dollars, for which one goes to prison, compared to financial speculations which deprive tens of millions of their homes and savings, and are then rewarded by state help of sublime grandeur? What is a Congolese local warlord compared to the enlightened and ecologically sensitive Western CEO? Maybe José Saramago was right when, in a 2008 newspaper column, he proposed treating the big bank managers and others responsible for the meltdown as perpetrators of crimes against humanity whose place is in the Hague Tribunal. Maybe one should not wave this proposal off as a poetic exaggeration in the style of Jonathan Swift, but take it seriously.

Taking into account this violence which is part of the normal functioning of global capitalism also compels us to throw a new light on its opposite, revolutionary terror. One should in no way cover up the harshness of the early Bolshevik rule – the point is elsewhere: precisely when they resorted to terror (and they often did it, openly calling the beast by its name: 'Red Terror'), this terror was of a different type from Stalinist terror. In Stalin's time, the symbolic status of the terror thoroughly changed – terror was turned into the publicly non-acknowledged, obscene, shadowy supplement to official discourse. It is significant that the climax of terror (1936–37) took place after the new constitution was accepted in 1935. This constitution was supposed to end the state of emergency and mark a return of things to normality: the suspension of the civil rights of whole strata of the population (kulaks, ex-capitalists) was rescinded, the right to vote was now universal, and so on and so forth. The key idea of this constitution was that now, after the stabilization of the socialist order and the annihilation of the enemy classes, the Soviet Union was no longer a class society: the subject of the state was no longer the working class (workers and peasants), but the people. However, this does not mean that the Stalinist constitution was a simple hypocrisy which concealed the social reality. To the contrary, the possibility of terror is inscribed into its very core: since the class war was proclaimed to be over and the Soviet Union was conceived of as the classless country of the People, those who opposed the regime (or were easily presumed to) became no longer 'class enemies' in a conflict that tore at the social body, but enemies of the People – insects, worthless scum to be excluded from humanity itself.

And far from concerning only the twentieth century, this topic retains its full actuality today. Alain Badiou recently proposed the formula of 'defensive violence': one should renounce violence (i.e. the violent takeover of state power) as the principal modus operandi, and rather focus on building free domains at a distance from state power, subtracted from its reign (like the early Solidarność in Poland), and only resort to violence when the state itself uses violence to crush and subdue these 'liberated zones'. The problem with this formula is that it relies on the deeply problematic distinction between the 'normal' functioning of state apparatuses and the 'excessive' exercise of state violence. Is not the first lesson in the Marxist notion of class struggle – or more precisely, on the priority of the class struggle over classes as positive social entities – the thesis that 'peaceful' social life is itself sustained by (state) violence, i.e.

that 'peace' is an expression and effect of the (temporary) victory or predominance of one class (namely the
ruling class) in the class struggle? What this means is
that one cannot separate violence from the very existence of the state (as the apparatus of class domination):
from the standpoint of the subordinated and oppressed,
the very existence of a state is a fact of violence (in the
same sense in which, for example, Robespierre said, in
his justification of the regicide, that one does not have
to prove that the king committed any specific crimes,
since the very existence of the king is a crime, an offence
against the freedom of the people). In this strict sense,
every violence of the oppressed against the ruling class
and its state is ultimately 'defensive'. If we do not concede this point, we *volens nolens* 'normalize' the state
and accept that its violence is merely a matter of contin-
gent excesses (to be dealt with through democratic
reforms). This is why the standard liberal motto apropos of violence – it is sometimes necessary to resort to
it, but it is never legitimate – is inadequate. From the
radical emancipatory perspective, one should turn this
motto around. For the oppressed, violence is always
legitimate (since their very status is the result of the violence they are exposed to), but never necessary (it is
always a matter of strategic consideration to use violence against the enemy or not).[5]

In short, the topic of violence should be demystified:
what was wrong with twentieth-century communism
was not its recourse to violence per se (the violent takeover of state power, terror in order to maintain power),
but rather the larger mode of functioning which made
this kind of violence inevitable and legitimized (the
party as the instrument of historical necessity, etc.). In
1970, in the notes of a meeting with President Richard
Nixon on how to undermine the democratically elected
Chilean government of Salvador Allende, CIA Director

---

5   I owe this idea to Udi Aloni.

Richard Helms wrote succinctly: 'Make the economy scream.' Top US representatives openly admit that today the same strategy is being applied in Venezuela: former US Secretary of State Lawrence Eagleburger said on Fox News that Chávez's appeal to the Venezuelan people

> only works so long as the populace of Venezuela sees some ability for a better standard of living. If at some point the economy really gets bad, Chávez's popularity within the country will certainly decrease and it's the one weapon we have against him to begin with and which we should be using, namely the economic tools of trying to make the economy even worse so that his appeal in the country and the region goes down . . . Anything we can do to make their economy more difficult for them at this moment is a good thing, but let's do it in ways that do not get us into direct conflict with Venezuela if we can get away with it.

The least one can say is that such statements give credibility to the suspicion that the economic difficulties faced by the Chávez government (major product and electricity shortages nationwide, etc.) are not only the result of the ineptness of its economic policies. Here we come to the key political point, which is difficult to swallow for some liberals: we are clearly not dealing here with blind market processes and reactions (say, shop owners trying to make more profit by keeping some products off the shelves), but with an elaborate and fully planned strategy – and in such conditions, is not a kind of terror (police raids on secret warehouses, detention of speculators and the coordinators of shortages, etc.), as a defensive countermeasure, fully justified? Even Badiou's formula of 'subtraction plus only reactive violence' seems inadequate in these new conditions. The problem today is that the state is getting more and more chaotic, failing in its proper function of 'servicing the goods', so that one cannot even afford to let the state do its job. Do we have the right to remain at a distance from state power when state power is itself disintegrating, turning into an obscene exercise of violence so as to mask its own impotence?

Instead of a simplistic rejection of violence and terror, one should thus first widen its scope – learn to see violence where the hegemonic ideology teaches us to see none – and then analyze it in a concrete way, detecting the potential emancipatory use of what may at first appear to be purely reactionary militarism. Let us take, from the sphere of great art, Shakespeare's *Coriolanus*, a play so exclusively focused on its hero's militaristic-aristocratic pride and contempt for ordinary people that one can easily see why, after the German defeat in 1945, the Allied occupation powers prohibited its performance. Consequently, the play seems to offer a rather narrow interpretive choice: what are the alternatives to staging the play the way it is, i.e. to surrendering to its militaristic anti-democratic lure? We can try to subtly 'extraneate' this lure by way of its excessive aestheticization; we can do what Brecht did in his rewriting of the play, shifting the focus from the display of emotions (Coriolanus' rage, etc.) to the underlying conflict of political and economic interests (in Brecht's version, the crowd and the tribunes are not lead by fear and envy, but act rationally in view of their situation); or, perhaps the worst choice, we can overplay pseudo-Freudian stuff about Coriolanus' maternal fixation and the homosexual intensity of his relationship with Aufidius. However, in the recent cinema version of the play, Ralph Fiennes (with his scenario writer John Logan) did the impossible, thereby perhaps confirming T. S. Eliot's famous claim that *Coriolanus* is superior to *Hamlet*: Fiennes broke out of this closed circle of interpretive options, which all introduce a critical distance towards the figure of Coriolanus, and

fully asserted Coriolanus – not as a fanatical anti-dem-
ocrat, but as a figure of radical Left.

Fiennes's first move was to change the geopolitical
coordinates of *Coriolanus*: 'Rome' is now a contemporary colonial city-state in crisis and decay, and the
'Volscians' Leftist guerrilla rebels organized in what
we call today a 'rogue state'. (Think of Colombia and
the FARC, the 'revolutionary armed forces of
Colombia' holding a vast territory in the south of the
country – if only the FARC had not been corrupted by
drug-dealing.) This first move echoes in many perspic-
uous details, like the decision to present the border
between the territory held by the Roman army and the
rebel territory, the place of contact between the two
sides, as a lone access ramp on a highway, a kind of
guerrilla checkpoint.[6]

One should fully exploit here the lucky choice of
Gerard Butler for the role of Aufidius, the Volscian
leader and Caius Martius's (i.e., Coriolanus's) oppo-
nent: since Butler's greatest hit was Zack Snyder's *300*,
where he played Leonidas, one should not be afraid to
venture the hypothesis that, in both films, he basically
plays the same role of a warrior-leader of a rogue state
fighting a mighty empire. *300*, the saga of the troop of
Spartan soldiers who sacrificed themselves at Thermo-
pylae to halt the invasion of Xerxes's Persian army,
was attacked as the worst kind of patriotic militarism
with clear allusions to the recent tensions with Iran and
events in Iraq. Are things really so clear, however? The
film should rather be thoroughly defended against
these accusations: it is the story of a small, poor country (Sparta) invaded by the vast armies of a much larger

---

6 One can dream further here: what about fully exploiting the
accidental fact that the film was shot in Serbia, with Belgrade as 'a city
that called itself Rome', and imagining the Volscians as Albanians from
Kosovo, with Coriolanus as a Serb general who changes side and joins
the Albanians?

state (Persia). At the time Persia was much more developed than the Peloponnese, and wielded much more impressive military technology – are not the Persians' elephants, giants and flaming arrows the ancient versions of today's high-tech weaponry? A programmatic statement towards the end of the film defines the Spartans' agenda as standing 'against the reign of mystique and tyranny, towards the bright future', which is further specified as the rule of freedom and reason. It sounds like an elementary Enlightenment programme, and with a communist twist! Also recall that, at the film's beginning, Leonidas rejects outright the message of the corrupt 'oracles' according to whom gods forbid the military expedition to stop the Persians. As we later learn, these 'oracles' who were allegedly receiving the divine message in an ecstatic trance were actually paid off by the Persians, like the Tibetan 'oracle' who, in 1959, delivered to the Dalai Lama the message to leave Tibet and who was – as we learn today – on the CIA payroll.

But what about the apparent absurdity of the Spartan idea of dignity, freedom and reason being sustained by extreme military discipline, including of the practice of discarding the weakest children? This 'absurdity' is simply the price of freedom – freedom is not free, as they put it in the film. Freedom is not something given; it is regained through a hard struggle in which one should be ready to risk everything. The Spartans' ruthless military discipline is not simply the external opposite of Athenian 'liberal democracy': such discipline is democracy's inherent condition, and lays the foundations for it. The free subject of reason can only emerge through ruthless self-discipline. True freedom is not 'freedom of choice' made from a safe distance – a consumer's choice. True freedom overlaps with necessity; one makes a truly free decision when one's choice puts at stake one's very existence – one does it because one simply 'cannot do otherwise'.

When one's country is undergoing a foreign occupation and one is called on by a resistance leader to join
the fight against the occupiers, the reason given is not
'you are free to choose', but: 'Can't you see that this is
the only thing you can do if you want to retain your
dignity?' No wonder that all the early modern egalitarian radicals – from Rousseau to the Jacobins – admired
Sparta and imagined republican France as a new
Sparta: there is an emancipatory core in the Spartan
spirit of military discipline which survives even when
we subtract all the historical paraphernalia of Spartan
class rule, ruthless exploitation of and terror over their
slaves, etc. Even Trotsky called the Soviet Union in the
difficult years of 'war communism' a 'proletarian
Sparta'.

So it is not that soldiers are the problem per se – the
real menace is soldiers *with poets*, soldiers mobilized by
nationalist poetry. There is no ethnic cleansing without
poetry – why? Because we live in an era which perceives
itself as post-ideological. Since great public causes no
longer have the force to mobilize people for mass violence, a larger sacred Cause is needed, a Cause which
makes petty individual concerns about killing seem triv-
ial. Religion or ethnic belonging fit this role perfectly.
And this brings us back to *Coriolanus* – who is the poet
there? Before Caius Martius (aka Coriolanus) enters the
stage, it is Menenius Agrippa who pacifies the furious
crowd which is demanding grain. Like Ulysses in *Troilus
and Cressida*, Menenius is the ideologist par excellence,
offering a poetic metaphor to justify social hierarchy (in
this case, the rule of the senate); and, in the best corpo-
ratist tradition, the metaphor is that of a human body.
Here is how Plutarch, in his *Life of Coriolanus*, retells
this story first reported by Livy:

> It once happened . . . that all the other members of a
> man mutinied against the stomach, which they accused
> as the only idle, uncontributing part in the whole body,

while the rest [of the members] were put to hardships
and the expense of much labour to supply and minister
to its appetites. The stomach, however, merely ridi-
culed the silliness of the members, who appeared not
to be aware that the stomach certainly does receive the
general nourishment, but only to return it again, and
redistribute it amongst the rest. Such is the case . . . ye
citizens, between you and the senate. The counsels and
plans that are there duly digested, convey and secure to
all of you your proper benefit and support.[7]

How does Coriolanus relate to this metaphor of body
and its organs, of the rebellion of organs against their
body? It is clear that, whatever Coriolanus is, he does
not stand for the body, but is an organ which not only
rebels against the body (the body politic of Rome), but
abandons its body by way of going into exile – a true
organ without a body. Is then Coriolanus really against
the people? But *which* people? The 'plebeians' represented by the two tribunes, Brutus and Sicinius, are not
any kind of exploited workers, but rather a lumpen-
proletarian mob, the rabble fed by the state; and the
two tribunes are proto-Fascist manipulators of the
mob – to quote Kane (the citizen from Welles's film),
they speak for the poor ordinary people *so that the
poor ordinary people will not speak for themselves*. If
one looks for 'the people', then, they are rather to be
found among the Volscians. One should watch closely
how Fiennes depicts their capital: a modest popular
city in a liberated territory, with Aufidius and his com-
rades in the uniforms of guerrilla fighters (not the
regular army) mixing freely with commoners in an
atmosphere of relaxed conviviality, with people drink-
ing in open-air cafeterias, etc. – in clear contrast to the
stiff formality of Rome.

---

7   *Plutarch's Lives of Illustrious Men*, vol. 1, trans. J. Dryden et al.,
New York: American Book Exchange, 1880, p. 340.

So yes, Coriolanus is a killing machine, a 'perfect soldier', but precisely as such, as an 'organ without a body', he has no fixed class allegiance and can easily put himself in the service of the oppressed. As was made clear by Che Guevara, a revolutionary also has to be a 'killing machine':

> Hatred [is] an element of the struggle; a relentless hatred of the enemy, impelling us over and beyond the natural limitations that man is heir to and transforming him into an effective, violent, selective, and cold killing machine. Our soldiers must be thus; a people without hatred cannot vanquish a brutal enemy.[8]

There are two scenes in the film which provide a clue for such a reading. When, after his violent outburst in the senate, Coriolanus exits the large hall and slams the doors behind him, he finds himself alone in the silence of a large corridor, confronted with an old tired cleaning man, and the two exchange glances in a moment of silent solidarity, as if only the poor cleaning man can see who Coriolanus is now. The other scene is a long depiction of his voyage into exile, done in a 'road movie' tenor, with Coriolanus as a lone rambler on his trek, anonymous among the ordinary people. It is as if Coriolanus, obviously out of place in the delicate hierarchy of Rome, only now becomes what he is, gains his freedom – and the only thing he can do to retain this freedom is to join the Volscians. He does not join them simply in order to take revenge on Rome, he joins them because he belongs there – it is only among the Volscian fighters that he can be what he is. Coriolanus's pride is authentic, joined with his reluctance to be praised by his compatriots and to engage in political manoeuvring. Such a pride has no place in Rome; it can thrive only among the guerrilla fighters.

---

8 Che Guevara, 'Message to the Tricontinental', in *Guerilla Warfare*, Lincoln, NE: University of Nebraska Press, 1998, p. 173.

In joining the Volscians, Coriolanus does not betray Rome out of a sense of petty revenge but regains his integrity – his only act of betrayal occurs at the end when, instead of leading the Volscian army onto Rome, he organizes a peace treaty between the Volscians and Rome, breaking down to the pressure of his mother, the true figure of superego Evil. This is why he returns to the Volscians, fully aware what awaits him there: the well-deserved punishment for his betrayal. And this is why Fiennes's *Coriolanus* is effectively like the saint's eye in an Orthodox icon: without changing a word in Shakespeare's play, it looks specifically at us, at our predicament today, outlining the unique figure of a radical freedom fighter.

So, back to Wahnich's book: the reader should approach its topic – terror and terrorism – without ideological fears and taboos, as a crucial contribution not only to the history of the emancipatory movements, but also as a reflection on our own predicament. Do not be afraid of its topic: the fear that prevents you from confronting it is the fear of freedom, of the price one has to pay for freedom.

ACKNOWLEDGEMENTS

Discussions at several different places gave rise to this little book. I have to thank Antoine de Baeque for having suggested that I take part in the study day he organized on the Terror in 1999, thus helping me to put these reflections into shape; Didier Fassin for having invited me to an interdisciplinary seminar on the notion of the intolerable; Alain Brossat for inviting me to a conference on terrorism; Arlette Farge for having encouraged me in my reflection on political emotions at the seminar she and Pierre Laborie organized on the event and its reception; and Marc Abélès for having opened up paths of anthropological reflection in the LAIOS seminar. My thanks also to those colleagues and friends, fellow historians of the French Revolution whom I joined in conducting a seminar on 'L'Esprit des Lumières et de la Révolution': Françoise Brunel, Yannick Bosc, Marc Deleplace, Florence Gauthier and Jacques Guilhaumou. My special thanks to Éric Hazan for having re-read the text of this essay with care and friendship. And thanks, finally, to Didier Leschi, who helped me so often to clarify my investigation by re-reading the different pieces of the puzzle as they came to light.

INTRODUCTION:
AN INTOLERABLE REVOLUTION

In Éric Rohmer's film *The Lady and the Duke* (2001), the French Revolution is seen through the eyes of Grace Elliott. This friend and former lover of the duc d'Orléans, before being imprisoned herself during the Terror, was confronted with two of those events that have given the Revolution its savage reputation: the massacres of September 1792 and the death of the king. During these massacres, Grace Elliott crossed Paris in a carriage. After having managed not to faint at the sight of the duchesse de Lamballe's head – whose well-known face was paraded in front of Elliott's carriage atop a pike – she cried in delayed shock when she reached her home and explained what she had seen. Faced with the impending death of the king, she hoped right until 21 January 1793 that the revolutionaries would not dare to kill him, and interpreted the cries of the people that she heard from her residence in Meudon as a demonstration to prevent his execution. After his death she went into mourning, and would not get over her anger at the duc d'Orléans, who had not only done nothing to oppose the king's death, but had actually voted for it. Revolutionary violence was imprinted on human bodies, whether in the institutional no man's land of the September massacres or in the context of the inventive institution of the king's trial. Grace

Elliott's reactions were both sensitive and moral: fear, anger and sadness are the expression of an emotional and normative judgement. We can well imagine that she found these two events 'insufferable'.

Elliott's point of view, which was also that of Edmund Burke and Hippolyte Taine, was expressed in the memoirs she later wrote and that were eventually published in 1859. But today, through the effect of this historical film, it has also become a contemporary point of view on the French Revolution.

If we cannot maintain that this vision of the Revolution is completely dominant today – since it is certainly not detested by all its heirs – we have to admit that the film's reception, both before and after its release in September 2001, was highly positive, not just on account of its aesthetic innovations but also for its ideological standpoint. Marc Fumaroli, in an article for *Cahiers du Cinéma* in July 2001, saw it as a key film on 'the bloodiest and most controversial days in our history',[1] and constructed a parallel between the prisons of the Terror and the Nazi-era extermination camps:

> When she meets up in prison with duchesses, coun-tesses, laundrywomen and actresses, all condemned to the scaffold for the mere fact of their birth or their allegiance, she is almost happy to share their fate, just as a 'goy' *résistante* would have been in the Drancy transit camp in 1942–43.[2]

We see here the conscious construction of a new recep-tion of the French Revolution which, out of disgust at the political crimes of the twentieth century, imposes an equal disgust towards the revolutionary event. The

---

1 Marc Fumaroli, 'Terreur et cinéma', *Cahiers du cinéma*, July–August 2001, p. 42.
2 Ibid., p. 44.

French Revolution is unspeakable because it constituted 'the matrix of totalitarianism' and invented its
rhetoric.[3]

The social and ideological cleavages that form the
fabric of the revolutionary event have constantly
plagued its representations. There have always been
counter-revolutionaries – and they were perceived as
such. Today, however, what is more surprising is
that these counter-revolutionary representations can
pass as majoritarian, commonplace, and – like Éric
Rohmer's film – be considered both by critics and the
public as historically correct. We are no longer in an
age in which different standpoints argue over an
event that resists interpretation, but rather one of
unquestioned detestation of the event. Since the
French Revolution includes what the British call the
'Reign of Terror', and the French simply 'the Terror',
not only can it no longer be seen as a historical movement which is redeemable en bloc, but it can in fact
be rejected en bloc. The French Revolution is a figure
of what is politically intolerable today, as it had
already become in 1795.

But is this disgust and rejection based on any reflec-
tive and critical stance? One small anecdote makes it
possible to doubt this. At the Sorbonne, allegedly the
stronghold of Jacobin historians, Michel Vovelle
replaced Albert Soboul in 1985. The following year he
offered to organize a 'calf's head dinner' for postgradu-
ates on 21 January. This is a traditional republican
ritual in which the calf's head represents the head of
the king: the people, gathered at a banquet, replay the
king's death in carnival mode. Vovelle's proposal met

---

3   Thus François Furet can write: 'Today the Gulag leads us to reflect
afresh on the Terror, by virtue of its identical project', and again:
'Solzhenitsyn's work . . . ineluctably locat[es] the issue of the Gulag at
the very core of the revolutionary endeavour.' *Interpreting the French
Revolution*, Cambridge: Cambridge University Press, 1978, p. 12.

with an icy reception. For the majority of students, even those enrolled in the Sorbonne's course on the history of the Revolution, it seemed indecent. The merry chuckling of Michel Vovelle was met by an embarrassed and incredulous silence. The calf's head ritual had become non-contemporary, without time being taken to assess it properly. It was impossible now to 'replay' the severed head – that kind of thing was shocking, or troubling at the least. To my mind, this collective banquet belongs to the 'obligatory expression of sentiments',[4] i.e. to 'a broad category of oral expressions of sentiments and emotions with a collective character':

> This in no way damages the intensity of these sentiments, quite the contrary ... but all these collective expressions, which have at the same time a moral value and an obligatory force for the individual and the group, are more than simple manifestations ... If they have to be told, it is because the whole group understands them. More than simply an expression of one's own sentiments, these are expressed to others, since they have to be expressed in this way. They are expressed to oneself by expressing them to others and for their benefit. This is essentially a matter of symbolism.[5]

This republican symbolism, however, came undone in the 1980s and 1990s. When the bicentennial celebration came round, the question of revolutionary violence returned to disturb some of the certainties that had newly imposed themselves since the Liberation. Until this time, the French had no need to be ashamed of the revolutionary event; they even had to be proud of it – proud of the French republican invention, a counter-model to the Vichy regime, and proud above

---

4   Marcel Mauss, *Essais de Sociologie*, Paris: Minuit, 1969, p. 88.
5   Ibid.

all of the Declaration of the Rights of Man and of the Citizen, which served as a reference point for the rebirth of international law and the famous Universal Declaration of Human Rights. At the time of the bicentenary of the French Revolution, however, 1789 and 1793 were disassociated, the challenge to the Ancien Régime was separated from the invention of the Republic – and in short, the wheat had been sorted from the chaff. 1789 was celebrated; but 1792, the fall of the monarchy and the invention of the Republic, remained in the shadow of Valmy. As for 1793, the preference was to merge its 'fine anticipations' with those of 1789. The abolition of slavery and the rights to education and public assistance were removed from their context without any investigation of how these irrefutable values were bound up with the Terror. Democracy in France today does not seem to sit well with its foundation. 'At a time when democracy has become the sole perspective of contemporary societies, it is essential for attention to focus on its inaugural moment, 1789, and not on the dark days of 1793', proclaimed Patrice Gueniffey,[6] one of the main current detractors of the Revolution, before going on to ask:

> Who would dare today to celebrate the Terror with the frankness of Albert Mathiez, who writes in 1922 that it was 'the red crucible in which the future democracy was elaborated on the accumulated ruins of everything associated with the old order'?[7]

In this vision, subsequent to the bicentenary but in the same spirit, democracy could no longer have anything to do with this 'red crucible'. The possibilities of appropriating the event today are encumbered by a sensitivity

---

6 Patrice Gueniffey, *La politique de la Terreur. Essai sur la violence révolutionnaire*, Paris: Fayard, 2000, p. 10.
7 Ibid.

to bloodshed, to political death meted out and decided: responsibly assumed.

By this evocation of blood, doubt is introduced as to the value of the revolutionary event. We have seen on magazine covers, and in productions for a wide audience, questions that might formerly have been thought peculiar to inveterate monarchists. 'Was it necessary to kill the king?', asks Le Nouvel Observateur in January 1993. 'Would you French television viewers of today have decided to kill the queen?', asks Robert Hossein at the end of his show about Marie-Antoinette. These questions have the value of interesting symptoms.

By applying the Kantian categorical imperative to judge past events, two hundred years after the facts, these questions involve people today in the historical situation of 1793. They have to put themselves in the place of the Convention members who actually had to judge this question, in the place of contemporaries of the event who had to discuss it and decide their political position. This amounts to inventing a mode of historicity that could be called the concatenation of presents, or of situations. Readers are no longer mere inheritors of an event in which they were not protagonists. If they do indeed want to be its heirs, then they are led to play a part in it. In other words, every heir of the republican foundation could be morally included in the category of regicides, or in what the Thermidorians called 'men of blood'. Who today, even among republicans, would assume such a designation? Kant's commentary on the French Revolution is familiar enough:

> The revolution of a gifted people which we have seen unfolding in our day may succeed or miscarry; it may be filled with misery and atrocities to the point that a sensible man, were he boldly to hope to execute it successfully the second time, would never resolve to attempt the experiment at such cost – this revolution, I

say, nonetheless finds in the hearts of all spectators (who are not engaged in this game themselves) a wishful participation that borders closely on enthusiasm, the very expression of which is fraught with danger; this sympathy, therefore, can have no other cause than a moral predisposition of the human race.[8]

Moral reverse projection onto the French Revolution, however, ends up making the position of a nonparticipating spectator impossible. Yet it is the 'play' of the actor – in both the theatrical and historical sense of the term – that is required in Robert Hossein's production. Here, too, spectators cannot remain spectators; they in fact become actors by voting for or against the death of Marie-Antoinette, and in this way collude in a simulacrum of popular consultation that leads to denying one of the very characteristics of the event, namely its irreversible character.

'To suggest putting Louis XVI on trial is a counterrevolutionary idea', Robespierre declared. 'It is making the Revolution itself a subject of litigation.'[9] And putting the king's trial on trial certainly means reopening such litigation; it explicitly means using the faculty of judgement rather than of understanding. The moral mechanism here stands in the way of historical curiosity. The object is no longer to understand the meaning of the death meted out to the man whom Saint-Just described as 'foreign' to humanity and the community. Nor is it to know what such an event succeeded in establishing, in terms of sovereignty. The question, rather, is settled in advance. What is played out here is the figure of *historical evil*, of the inability

---

8 Immanuel Kant, *The Conflict of the Faculties*, trans. M. J. Gregor, New York: Abaris Books, 1979, p. 153.
9 Robespierre, *Pour le Bonheur et pour la Liberté, Discours*, ed. Yannick Bosc, Florence Gauthier and Sophie Wahnich, Paris: Éditions La Fabrique, 2000, p. 194.

to settle political conflicts peacefully – i.e. without inflicting violence on the body, without putting to death. To be a happy heir to the French Revolution means becoming complicit with a historical crime. The event's character as a political laboratory is thus eroded in favour of a moral question. Scholarly historical debate – in the historicist sense of the term – becomes a forbidden zone. The decontextualizing and naturalizing of the sentiment of 'humanity' are made to reign in the eternal present of a moral condemnation.

This replay of the event in the mode of judgement – moral and normative, sensible and emotional, in a context of aestheticization – leads the Revolution to appear insufferable to the very people who, in terms of classic political sociology, are not supposed to be its detractors. From now on the Revolution finds critics not only just on the right of the French political spectrum but also on the left, among the heirs of Jean Jaurès and the Socialist International.

UNDER CROSS-EXAMINATION:
ARGUMENTS FOR THE PROSECUTION

This new disgust with the French Revolution is inseparable from a 'parallel' constructed with the history of political catastrophes in the twentieth century, and from a related idealization of the present democratic model of politics. It is the impact of this democratic model, which is presented as a culminating point in the process of civilization, that makes possible this charge against the French Revolution. Whereas contemporary democracy protects the individual, the Revolution protected the sovereign people as a political and social group; whereas our democracy institutionalizes a third arbitrating power – the *Conseil constitutionnel* – between the people and their representation, the Revolution gave all power to the elected assembly; whereas democratic conflict is now supposed to be based on a politics made up of compromise, approximations and calculations, the Revolution dreamed of an absolute politics, illusory and utopian, resting on principles; whereas democratic justice is penal, and restricted by positive law, revolutionary justice is political, resting on social vengeance and the idealism of natural right. Contrasts of this kind, as presented in the arguments of the detractors of the revolutionary political model, could be multiplied *ad libitum*.[10]

Disgust and idealization are thus the two emotional faces of the construction of a Revolution as the *other* to democracy. And the sum total of political and social forms qualified as revolutionary and totalitarian can then be amalgamated in a common rejection.

This confused analogy finds a more precise and radical formulation in certain contemporary philosophical analyses. Giorgio Agamben, in *Homo Sacer*, expresses it in these terms:

> The idea of an inner solidarity between democracy and totalitarianism (which here we must, with every caution, advance) is obviously not . . . a historiographical claim, which would authorize the liquidation and levelling of the enormous differences that characterize their history and their rivalry. Yet this idea must nevertheless be strongly maintained on a historico-philosophical level, since it alone will allow us to orient ourselves in relation to the new realities and unforeseen convergences of the end of the millennium.[11]

---

10   I have in mind here the works of Marcel Gauchet, *La Révolution des pouvoirs*, Paris: Gallimard, 1995; and Ladan Boroumand, *La Guerre des principes*, Paris: Éditions de l'EHESS, 1999.
11   Giorgio Agamben, *Homo Sacer: Sovereign Power and Bare Life*, trans. Daniel Heller-Roazen, Palo Alto, CA: Stanford University Press, 1998, p. 10.

The French Revolution, as the alleged founding moment of our Western democracies, is implicitly targeted by this thesis. The historiographical dimension of this criticism is still more explicit in Agamben's *Means Without End*: '[In] all the declarations of rights from 1789 to the present day . . . the state makes nativity or birth (that is, naked human life) the foundation of its own sovereignty.'[12] And the historical parallel between revolution and totalitarianism is made still more explicit in an article titled 'Qu'est-ce qu'un peuple?', in which Agamben maintains that

> starting with the French Revolution, sovereignty is entrusted solely to the people, the *people* become an embarrassing presence, and poverty and exclusion appear for the first time as an intolerable scandal in every sense . . . From this perspective, our time is nothing other than the methodical and implacable attempt to fill the split that divides the people by radically eliminating the people of the excluded.[13]

Since we know that, for Agamben, this absence of division among the people leads to the fantasy of a pure, homogeneous, unified people, as in the Nazi notion of *Volk*, this can only be disturbing. In the end, this philosopher rediscovers the thesis of a theoretical matrix common both to totalitarianism and to the contemporary democracies, which can be analyzed in the founding event that is the French Revolution. This is the theoretical matrix of biopolitics, which he claims is inscribed at the heart of the sovereign power of the revolutionary period.

Michel Foucault had already opposed the pair of

---

12   Giorgio Agamben, 'Beyond Human Rights', in *Means Without End: Notes on Politics*, trans. V. Binetti and C. Casarino, Minneapolis: University of Minnesota Press, 2000, p. 20.
13   Agamben, 'What Is a People?', in *Means Without End*, p. 33.

actions that characterized the sovereign power –
'making die' and 'letting live' – to the pair characterizing
what he called biopolitics – 'making live' and 'letting
die'. Such a politics, for him, assumed that 'the species
and the individual as a simple living body become what
is at stake in a society's political strategies'.[14] 'What
follows is a kind of bestialization of man achieved
through the most sophisticated political techniques . . .
and at once it becomes possible both to protect life and
to authorize a holocaust.'[15]

This is the point from which Agamben's reflections
begin. Far from supporting this opposition between
biopolitics and sovereignty, he maintains that both the
sovereign exception's practice of 'making die' and the
biopolitical practices described by Foucault involve
the production of a 'biopolitical body'. This body is
then an object of power, corresponding to the other
side of the Greek *zoē*, animal life as opposed to *bios*,
to political or properly human life inasmuch as this is
a life of liberty guided by the idea of a collective good
life in the community. For Agamben, 'the exception
everywhere becomes the rule . . . right and fact enter
into a zone of irreducible indistinction'.[16] The extermination camp is the place par excellence where the
biopolitical body is formed, and where the state of
exception is the only right.

The end point of this long line of argument is that
the question asked about the French Revolution indi-
cates a profound solidarity between democratic and
totalitarian regimes, a political foundation at which
there is no longer a difference between animal life and
political life. But is this at all tenable? Is the French
Revolution, and the Terror in particular, part and

---

14   Agamben, *Homo Sacer*, p. 3.
15   Michel Foucault, *Dits et écrits, vol. 2: 1954–88*, Paris: Gallimard,
1994, p. 719; cited by Agamben in *Homo Sacer*, p. 3.
16   Agamben, *Homo Sacer*, p. 9.

parcel of this zone of irreducible non-differentiation? And if yes, how so? Finally – and this question is fundamental – did the revolutionary effort aim to let this zone of non-differentiation expand without limits, in the way that historians have spoken for example of unbounded suspicion, or did it aim on the contrary to maintain this as a marginal place in the political organization?

This biopolitical body, used to undermine the French Revolution, had also been denounced earlier by Hannah Arendt in her essay *On Revolution*, if without using the new term. The social question and the formulation of a right to existence were in her view the inaugural forms of a politics in which the question of 'life', as she called it (Aristotle's *zoē*, Agamben's 'bare life'), acquired full right in the field of politics, inaugurating a politics of pity. By denouncing social inequality between rich and poor, the revolutionaries, according to Arendt, destroyed the possibility of a politics based not on the principle of equality but rather on that of liberty. For her, in effect, what was at issue in politics was not life but the world. Liberty was a reality of the world that existed in a common space that men inserted themselves into by action and speech. Men are free when they act. For Arendt, the social question led the Revolution to produce men who, instead of being free and citizens, would be equals in the relationship established to material goods, and reduced – just as under the denounced Ancien Régime – to the state of a flock of animals. In this context of arithmetic equalization, no one would seek any more to act on the world, and all that mattered would be to maintain 'the beautiful day of life', as Aristotle put it.[17] Contrary to what was asserted in the Declaration of Rights, they would be

---

17 [At 1278b in the *Politics*, Aristotle uses the term *euēmeria*, literally 'beautiful day' but variously translated as 'serenity', 'comfort', and 'well-being' – D. F.]

living men who did not manage to rise to the state of citizens.

For Arendt, the question of the blood spilled by the revolutionaries, of cruelty towards the political enemy, was bound up with the entry of the 'unfortunate' onto the stage in 1793–94: 'Pity, seen as the wellspring of virtue, was claimed to possess a higher potential for cruelty than that of cruelty itself.' Arendt cites the most radical of the revolutionaries, 'Out of pity, out of love for humanity, be inhuman', and she continues:

> These words are the authentic language of passion, followed by the crude but none the less precise and very widespread justification of the cruelty of pity; the skilled and kindly surgeon uses his cruel and charitable knife to cut off the gangrened limb and thus save the body of the patient.[18]

In this way, the French Revolution becomes an intolerable historical event, one which injures a general present-day sensitivity by offering the archetype of a violence inflicted and assumed on the body of the enemy, and an imaginary of cruelty at once exceptional and unbounded, since it is legitimated in the minds of those who perform it by their sentiment of doing good.

Aversion to the French Revolution combines rejection of a politics of pity that produces political impotence with rejection of a politics of cruelty bound up with the passion for the unfortunate and the exercise of the sovereign exception. As Giorgio Agamben concludes:

> until a completely new politics . . . no longer founded on the *exceptio* of bare life – is at hand . . . the 'beautiful day' of life will be given citizenship only either

18 Hannah Arendt, *On Revolution*, Harmondsworth: Penguin, 1990, pp. 79–80.

through blood and death or in the perfect senselessness
to which the society of the spectacle condemns it.[19]

These theoretical issues offer a further step towards
understanding how aversion for the Republic can draw
in the whole of the socio-political spectrum. It is no
longer simply with respect to the supposed perfection
of the present democratic model that the Revolution is
intolerable, but also with respect to what the articulation of its legacy – modern sovereignty – and its
inventiveness – the project of a just and happy society
– have supposedly produced: political impotence.

In order to reopen these debates, it is necessary to
return to the archives, to the nitty-gritty of the revolutionary political and philosophical project. A return to
certain key moments of what is customarily known as
the revolutionary dynamic will make it possible to cast
a new light on the political and historical link between
liberty, sovereignty and equality, and to offer a new
interpretation.

EXPELLING DREAD: NEW QUESTIONS ABOUT THE TERROR

'But what can have struck men so greatly that they kill
their own kind, not with the amoral and unreflective
act of the semi-animal barbarian who follows his
instincts without knowing anything else, but under an
impulse of conscious life, as creator of cultural forms?'[20]
This question was formulated in order to try to raise
the veil over the mystery of rituals of sacrifice, and it is
tempting to apply it to the period of the Terror.

In fact, this explicitly anthropological approach
makes it possible to take a distance from any a priori
judgement on the Terror, and to associate three terms

---

19   Agamben, *Homo Sacer*, p. 11.
20   I take this question from Adolphe Jensen, *Mythes et coutumes des
peuples primitifs*, Paris: Payot, 1954, pp. 206–207.

that today have become unpronounceable together: 'terror', 'culture', and 'impulse of creative life'. Such an inquiry will reopen the dossier on a cause that seems to be satisfactorily understood and closed – that of the reasons for the violence of the Terror. Rejecting the other, more implicit anthropology, which fuels the dominant historical discourse and steers it towards notions of impulses, barbarism and instinct, of the deadly tendency bound up with a 'rigourism of virtue',[21] we might hope to resolve the question of foundational violence.[22]

If it is nothing new to analyze the Terror in terms of foundational violence, this very idea of *foundation* is always bound up with the struggle against the Ancien Régime and is never made any more specific.[23] A violence of this kind, however, can be rehabilitated without considering it as directed specifically against the Ancien Régime. Various religious rituals com-memorate times of foundation and symbolically handle the risks of violence bound up with a moment that combines the destruction and the construction of social ties, risks that can indeed lead to the demise of

---

21   An expression that serves as the subject of Françoise Brunel's article 'Le jacobinisme, un "rigorisme de la vertu"?', in *Mélanges offerts à Michel Vovelle. Sur la Révolution, approches plurielles*, Paris: Société des Études Robespierristes, 1997, pp. 271–80, where she criticizes among other things the psychoanalytic approach of Jacques André in *La Révolution fratricide. Essai de psychanalyse du lien social*, Paris: PUF, 1993.

22   The question is indeed to rediscover and give new legitimacy to the object that Colin Lucas particularly focused on in his intervention at the Stanford conference on terror, 'Revolutionary Violence, the People and the Terror', which can be found in K. M. Baker (ed.), *The French Revolution and the Creation of Modern Political Cultures, vol. 4: The Terror*, Oxford: Pergamon Press, 1994, pp. 57–80.

23   The article on 'Terror' in the *Dictionnaire historique de la Révolution française*, for example, states that 'the Terror was initially an effort to limit and define the legal field conceded to the foundational violence of the revolution against the Ancien Régime . . . this violence proved its salvation'; article by Claude Mazauric, Paris: PUF, 1989, p. 1024.

the community. It is these same risks that make it possible to understand and analyze the Terror as foundation. This very exercise, however, is not without its risks.

The first of these is to view the Terror as a resurgence of primitivism. Yet political anthropologists' use of the primitive society/modern society opposition does not seem to me an adequate response.[24] Drawing on the investigations of anthropologists cannot today lead to negating a society's historicity. Founding is not a primitive act, though we can hypothesize that there are anthropological analogies in the act of foundation – whether this occurs in the fifth, the eighteenth or the twentieth century. It is also worth recalling here that eighteenth-century anthropology did not merely distinguish between primitive and modern peoples, but also between free peoples and slave peoples; yet 'primitive' does not coincide with 'slave', nor 'modern' with 'free'. History was then often seen as a procedure of denaturing that led free peoples into slavery – thus adding to the critique of the 'primitive society/modern society' dichotomy.

The second risk is to propose an analysis in 'theologico-political' terms. One approach of this kind has already been radically criticized.[25] The particular 'theologico-political' in question here is one that posited the power of religious principles, and Catholicism in particular, in order to interpret such secular revolutionary notions as 'virtue'. Michel Vovelle emphasized the path taken towards secularism by the French revolutionaries, as opposed to the English revolutionaries who had still needed the

---

24   Cf. in particular Marc Abélès and Henri-Pierre Jeudy, *Anthropologie du politique*, Paris: Armand Colin, 1997. These authors maintain in their introduction: 'Essentially, anthropology can completely dispense with the notion of modernity' (p. 17).

25   Brunel, 'La jacobinisme, un "rigorisme de la vertu"?'

Bible in order to act.[26] It is true that the question of a sacred bond was far from absent from the revolutionaries' concerns. To 're-bind' (*religare*) men by sacred bonds was an important aspect of the revolutionary project of year II. But the question of foundation is not a theologico-political one. The notion of a 'transfer of sacredness', proposed by Mona Ozouf in order to explain the investment of a secular political sphere by people who were familiar with the imbrication of religious and political power, muddied the waters.[27] The invention of a new sacred sphere, in fact, does not presuppose shifting the symbolic and emotional investments of religion towards politics, but rather of adding the two together by offering individuals a different site for their desires for community. Civic religion is another possible way of combining people. If this seemed necessary to the revolutionaries, it was not exclusive. The question, then, is to grasp what political sacrality, as foundation of a circulation of emotions, led to the violence of the Terror in the build-up to year II.[28]

I have chosen here the paradigm of emotions, and not, as might have been expected for the eighteenth century, that of passions or moral sentiments. Despite not being contemporary with the Revolution, the notion of emotion has the advantage of highlighting an 'upsurge' that combines a state of the body and a judgement,[29] i.e. feeling and judging at

---

26 Michel Vovelle, particularly in *La Mentalité révolutionnaire. Société et mentalités sous la révolution française*, Paris: Éditions Sociales, 1985.
27 Mona Ozouf's expression deserves also to be applied empirically: if there is a transfer of sacrality, what mechanisms does this involve?
28 Bronislaw Baczko, in his contribution 'The Terror Before the Terror?', emphasized the fact that under Thermidor, as again in today's historiography, 'there is no consensus on a date or event that would symbolize the beginning of the terror'; in Baker (ed.), *The Terror*, p. 22.
29 Cf. in particular, Patricia Paperman and Ruwen Ogien (eds) *La*

the same time. This was indeed what the protagonists of the Terror expected of a good revolutionary.
Saint-Just, when depicting the events of 26 Germinal
of year II, proposed a combination of mind and
heart:

> The man of revolution is merciless to the bad, but he
> is sensitive, he pursues the guilty in the tribunals and
> defends innocence, he speaks the truth so that it will
> instruct, and not so that it offends . . . His probity is
> not a delicacy of spirit but a quality of the heart.
> Honour the mind but base yourselves on the heart.[30]

Besides, approaching the Terror from the side of the
emotions makes it possible to distinguish between the
violence triggered by the circulation of discourse,[31] and
that triggered by the rupture of a conscious or unconscious sacred equilibrium. Patrice Gueniffey, borrowing
the concept of a 'cumulative radicalization of discourse' from Hans Mommsen, who coined it in relation
to National Socialism, maintains:

> As soon as it is formulated, any definition of the
> Revolution is exposed to the competition of other defi-
> nitions that deepen its nature and radicalize its
> objectives. In this lies the motor of that revolutionary
> dynamic which, escalating in the definition of ends and
> the choice of means, leads inexorably to violence by
> way of a process of cumulative radicalization of dis-
> course.[32]

---

couleur des pensées, sentiments, émotions, intentions, Paris: EHESS,
1995.
30   *Archives parlementaires*, vol. 88, p. 615.
31   What Jean-Pierre Faye called 'the blow of discourse within a
narrative economy' in *Langages totalitaires. Critique de la raison de
l'économie narrative*, Paris: Hermann, 1972.
32   Gueniffey, *La Politique de la Terreur*, p. 230.

Far, however, from viewing the Terror as based on this kind of dynamic of narrative economy which aimed at the liquidation of an enemy to be overthrown, I shall put forward the hypothesis of a founding dynamic of emotional economy, one that arises from the sacred and from vengeance.[33] In this context, the revolutionaries had both to understand the risks of violence and dislocation of society bound up with the rapid circulation of emotions, and to control these by the symbolic activity of which discourse is part – in particular, the discourse of law.

What put the Terror on the agenda, as we know, was a new declaratory turn. Faced with the intent of the counter-revolutionaries to terrorize the patriots, the latter replied: 'Let us be terrible.'[34] This turn has been interpreted in terms of a 'terror-response'.[35] Both of these combined terms are suggestive, as it was

33   For this definition of vengeance as a foundational institution, see Pierre Bonte and Michel Izard (eds), *Dictionnaire de l'ethnologie et de l'anthropologie*, Paris: PUF, 1992, p. 738. As opposed to Arno Mayer in *The Furies* (Princeton: Princeton University Press, 2001), I do not disassociate analysis of vengeance and the sacred, and take seriously the idea of vengeance as a public institution rather than an individual passion. This notion of vengeance is therefore not analyzed as a vicious circle, but rather as the possibility of a virtuous institution. On Mayer's book, see *French Historical Studies*, vol. 24, no. 4 (2001), which was devoted to it, and where, among other contributions, there are interesting points of view from Tim Tackett and David Bell.

34   A rigorous description of this declaratory turn has been conducted by Jacques Guilhaumou in his article 'La terreur à l'ordre du jour (juillet 1793–mars 1794)', *Dictionnaire des usages sociopolitiques (1770–1815). Fascicule 2: Notions, concepts*, Paris: Klincksieck Inalf, 1987, pp. 127–60.

35   Mona Ozouf, 'Guerre et Terreur dans le discours révolutionnaire', *L'École de la France*, Paris: Gallimard, 1984, pp. 109–27. We might very well just use the term used repeatedly by the revolutionaries of a terror-vengeance, since we know that vengeance often includes a demand for reparatory equality, adding however that this demand may also be more absolute when the question is to avenge the dead or the integrity and dignity of man as this is instituted by a particular culture.

precisely a question of response, in the sense of finding a new voice after a sense of annihilation. Response is not like a simple rebound in which the ball is sent back across the net: it is rather a question of a resumption, in the sense in which a subject recovers and thus takes 'the initiative of terror'.[36] And the notion of emotional economy strikes me as particularly pertinent for analyzing the modalities of this resumption, since this return or resumption can be described not as a mere shift in utterance, but rather as a shift in emotions, from 'being terrorized' to 'being in anger' and 'being terrifying' – or more precisely, as a transcending of 'agitation' (*émoi*). This French word *émoi* derives from the earlier *esmayer*, meaning 'to disturb, frighten, deprive someone of their strength, discourage'. This verb also means to take someone out of themselves by casting a spell. *Émoi* is therefore a generic figure of fright, and thus deadly. Far from presupposing an immediate response, it implies for those who feel it a high risk of demise.

The question, 'How was Terror put on the agenda?' should thus be replaced by the question, 'How was the dread instilled in the revolutionaries by their enemies overcome and transformed into the demand for terror?' And beyond this, how was this demand was understood and accepted? And finally, what did the Terror found, or seek to found?

---

36   This is the expression found in the documentary record.

1

THE EMOTIONS IN THE
DEMAND FOR TERROR

SUBLIME DREAD: WELLSPRING OF THE SACRED

In the summer of 1793, the death of Marat aroused a feeling of dread in the people of Paris. This dread was initially sublimated in the form taken by Marat's funeral ceremony, before being turned into a popular demand for vengeance and terror.[1] Around Marat's corpse, which represented the injured people and the Declaration of the Rights of Man and of the Citizen, feelings of affliction and grief were transformed into enthusiasm. Spectators of the event moved from a palpable sense of discouragement to a feeling of enthusiasm towards 'the spirit of Marat'. His burial was accompanied by the declaration that 'Marat is not dead'. This proclaimed that the Revolution had not been destroyed, and would not be so. It then became possible to demand vengeance, and put terror on the agenda. This movement, which Jacques Guilhaumou describes in terms of the aesthetics of politics,[2] involved not simply the dis-

---

1 Jacques Guilhaumou, *La Mort de Marat*, Brussels: Complexe, 1989.
2 On aesthetics and politics, compare the works of Jacques Guilhaumou that relate Kantian aesthetics and the revolutionary process. For an analysis of the death of Marat in this light, see the very

position of bodies, the circulation of emotions and sentiments that inspired them, but also, as I see it, the relationship established to a sacred object.

In fact, if the bloodied body of Marat produced such disarray, it was because, by embodying the Declaration of the Rights of Man and of the Citizen, this was a sacred body, and its assassination a severe profanation. The question then was to re-establish the aura of sacredness around Marat's decomposing body, which the funeral ceremony did by transposing sentiments from the body to the 'spirit', from the embodied meaning to the symbolized meaning of 'Marat'. We could say, in the language of the Revolution, that this ceremony secured public safety by re-establishing the power of enthusiasm for right, in place of the affliction felt towards the dead body. Because the body was sacred, its death produced dread; but because this sacredness was based on a text proclaimed under the auspices of the Supreme Being, it could become a point of support for regaining the initiative.

(I use the notion of 'sacred' here without giving it a precise prior meaning. The composite definition given by anthropology, in fact, allows us to avoid fixing it in a single denotation, and in this way to introduce different aspects of it that are pertinent to the revolutionary period. Durkheim's analytic definition, according to which the sacred is what is protected by prohibitions, seems essential to me in order to conceive the question

---

clear presentation 'Fragment d'une esthétique de l'événement révolutionnaire', in Gilles Suron, Andrej Turowski and Sophie Wahnich (eds), *L'Art et le discours face à la Révolution*, Dijon: EUD, 1997; as well as 'Un changement du souveraineté et de sensibilité', in *L'avènement des porte-parole de la république, 1789–1792*, Villeneuve d'Ascq: Presses Universitaires du Septentrion, 1998, pp. 249–53. Also Jacques Rancière, *Disagreement: Politics and Philosophy*, trans. Julie Rose, Minneapolis: University of Minnesota Press, 1999; and *The Politics of Aesthetics: The Distribution of the Sensible*, trans. Gabriel Rockhill, London: Continuum, 2004.

of the boundary that if crossed makes someone an enemy, or the boundary to be re-established so as to avoid being destroyed by boundless dread. But the sacred in the sense of Hubert and Mauss, a transcendent reality that can be experienced, is also useful to grasp experiences such as funeral ceremonies. When this transcendence is nothing other than the society itself, and the sacred/profane opposition is combined with that of society/individual, this sacred can be given the name of 'value', as it is with Louis Dumont. We are then very close to the situation in the Revolution, where the sacred was essentially immanent.)

With the death of Marat, therefore, it was the transaction between sacred body and sacred text that made it possible to resist the enemies of the Revolution and to sublimate dread. This type of transaction recurs throughout the revolutionary period. It arises time and again whenever public safety is at stake, which is another way of saying, whenever dread risks dissolving the revolutionary social and political bond.

The notion of public safety runs right through the Revolution, and gives a name to a situation of extremity in which the safety of the people is the supreme law. Since this supreme law finds its theoretical foundation in the body of rules of natural right, its evocation serves to produce, around dread, the aura of the sacredness of right.[3] But appealing to the sacred is not sufficient for public safety; it has also to be enacted. And enacting it always means engaging bodies to rescue right as the condition of liberty. Formulas such as 'liberty or death' have to be understood literally: they express a transaction that passes via the sacrifice of the body. The first oaths of the National Guard are quite explicit on this point. That taken in 1789 by the *fédérés* of the Guerche ran:

---

3   On this question of natural right, see Florence Gauthier, *Triomphe et mort du droit naturel en Révolution*, Paris: PUF, 1992.

We, military citizens of the towns and countryside that
form the district of the Guerche, swear on our arms
and our honour to be loyal to the nation, the laws, and
the king . . . to maintain the constitution with all our
power, to be ever united in the closest friendship, to
assemble at the first sign of common danger, to support one another and our brother *fédérés* on every
occasion, to die if need be in order to defend liberty,
the first right of man, and the sole foundation of the
happiness of nations, and to regard as irreconcilable
enemies of God, nature and man those who seek to
undermine our rights and our liberty.[4]

From 1789 on, therefore, these oaths inscribed the def-
initions of friend and enemy in the order of the sacred.
This enemy is irreconcilable because he infringes the
sacred order, in which God, nature and men are very
clearly associated. It was by affirming their determina-
tion to die to defend the laws and rights of the French
that the *fédérés* considered themselves defending a
sacred order. Each time that dread surged up, the question for the people was to save themselves by committing
themselves in a sacred fashion, what could be called
'body and soul'.

This same will to commitment is evident in the
many addresses and petitions drawn up by the popular societies in May and June 1792, demanding a
declaration that 'the *patrie* is in danger'. The word
patrie made it possible to name the place of liberty
and laws. Saint-Just thus asserted: 'Where there are
no laws, there is no longer a *patrie*.'[5] To 'die for the
laws', then, became 'to die for the endangered *patrie*'.
Addresses, deputations and petitions, which

4   Arch. Nat., série C, carton 118, Creuse.
5   L.A. de Saint-Just, 'Esprit de la Révolution et de la Constitution,
1791', in *Œuvres complètes*, ed. Michèle Duval, Paris: Champ Libre,
1984, pp. 338–9.

expressed public opinion and transformed diffuse rumour into political assertion, declared that the 'dread' provoked not only by war but also by the treason of the king – and in particular his perjury, which was likewise a profanation of sacred rule – had to be countered. For example:

> A large number of citizens from the Luxembourg section cannot regard without dread the terrible situation in which the French empire now stands. The enemy is at the gates. Fanatics are conspiring within. The seditious, writhing in all directions, are profiting from all possible circumstances to achieve the terrible work they have been plotting for a long time. The king swore to be the father, the support of all the French, and he is exposing them to destruction.[6]

The transition from dread to defensive action ran by way of implementing the proclamation that 'the *patrie* is in danger'.[7] What was involved here was the opening of the National Guard to 'passive citizens', and the possibility for each person to participate in this sacred transaction – to offer their body to rescue the people and the Revolution, to save right.

Response thus presupposes the wellspring of the sacred produced by the relationship between the event and the Declaration of Rights, a relationship committing the bodies of the revolutionary actors, ready to die in order to save the revolutionary project because this was identified with the Declaration of the Rights of

---

6 *Archives parlementaires*, vol. 45, p. 352 (19 June 1792).
7 The emphasis is mine. On the function of this statement, see S. Wahnich, 'De l'émotion souveraine à l'acte de discours souverain, la patrie en danger', in *Mélanges offerts à Michel Vovelle*, Paris: Société des études Robespierristes, 1997. See also Jacques Comaille, Laurence Dumoulin and Cécile Robert, 'Produire les normes en Révolution', *Droit et société 7: La juridicisation du politique*, Paris: Maison des Science de l'Homme et Réseau Européen Droit et Société, 2000.

Man and of the Citizen. This is why the notion of *vengeance*, one of the modalities of expression of resentment towards enemies, and likewise that of *punishment*, always come up when public safety is at stake. On 12 August 1793, for example, when Royer demanded the raising of 'the terrible mass of sans-culottes', Danton replied:

> The deputies of the primary assemblies have come to exercise among us the initiative of terror against domestic enemies. Let us respond to their wishes. No amnesty for any traitor. The just man does not show mercy to the evil. Let us signal popular vengeance on the conspirators within by the sword of the law.[8]

The demand for terror was inseparable from the *levée en masse* demanded by Royer. As for the revolutionary army,[9] as a popular army it was the site par excellence of the transaction between the sacred body of the patriot, the law that was sacred by definition, and the sacred body of the impure enemy. On 5 September 1793, an exchange between the movers of the address drafted by Hébert and Royer and the president of the Assembly, who was none other than Robespierre, displayed this immediate relationship of the citizens to the exercise of sovereignty, as both a military exercise and an exercise of justice:

> It is time that equality waved its scythe over all heads. It is time to terrify all conspirators. Very well, then, legislators, put terror on the agenda. Let us be in revolution, since our enemies hatch counter-revolution

---

8   *Le Moniteur universel*, vol. 17, pp. 387–8; reprinted Paris: Plon, 1947.
9   This revolutionary army should not be confused with the regular armies: accompanied by a 'holy' guillotine, it was to give force to the law, struggle against embezzlers and supply the armies.

everywhere. Let the sword of the law hover over all the guilty. We demand the establishment of a revolutionary army, divided into several sections, each followed by a fearsome tribunal and the terrible instrument of the vengeance of the laws.

Robespierre then replied to the delegation: 'Citizens, it is the people who have made the revolution, and it is up to you to ensure the execution of the prompt measures needed to save the *patrie* . . .'[10]

To demand that terror be placed on the agenda meant demanding a politics aimed at constantly renewing this sacred character of the laws, permanently reaffirming the normative value of the Declaration of Rights, demanding vengeance and punishment for the enemies of the *patrie*. The slogan '*patrie en danger*' and the watchword 'terror' were launched by the people. Sovereign emotions coined sovereign slogans, with terror perhaps being seen as 'one of the modalities by which the popular appropriation of sovereignty is effected'.[11] Citizens asserted their sovereignty by demanding to be the first agents of public safety.

Far from being signs of a death-dealing tendency, these demands were the sign of a movement of life and enthusiasm.[12] They transmuted the dissolving emotions produced throughout the social body by acts of profanation into emotions that gave new courage. Thus, on the revolutionary *journée* of 20 June 1792, the faubourg Saint-Antoine came en masse to

---

10   *Le Moniteur universel*, vol. 17, p. 526.
11   Guéniffey, *La politique de la Terreur*, p. 197.
12   The description of this tendency is often taken from Hegel: 'The sole work and deed of universal freedom is therefore death, a death too which has no inner significance or filling, for what is negated is the empty point of the absolutely free self. It is thus the coldest and meanest of all deaths, with no more significance than cutting off a head of cabbage or swallowing a mouthful of water.' See *Phenomenology of Spirit*, trans. A. V. Miller, Oxford: Oxford University Press, 1977, para. 590.

the Tuileries, exchanged toasts with the king and made him wear the red cap of liberty. It was a symbolic victory of little substance, since even so the king did not ratify the decrees that aimed at the defence of Paris and its revolutionary gains – decrees that he had already vetoed.[13] But this *journée* was also when the faubourg explicitly demanded that the Assembly should declare the *patrie* to be in danger. Santerre, in his speech to the Assembly, reaffirmed this ability to regain the energy of liberty in action when what was sacred was in danger:

> Do the enemies of the *patrie* imagine that the men of 14 July have gone to sleep? If they appeared to be so, their awakening is terrible. They have lost nothing of their energy. The immortal Declaration of the Rights of Man is too deeply engraved in their hearts. This precious treasure will be defended by them, and nothing will be capable of stealing it from them.[14]

In order to understand the emotional economy of the demand for terror, we do not have to ask whether the obsession with plots was really well-founded, and how the revolutionary sacrality that had been produced was being flouted. What effectively instilled dread was this rupture of the sacred.

It remains to be understood how this movement of enthusiasm that demanded vengeance did not produce a 'fury of destruction'[15] in the sense of a generalized massacre, but led to the establishment of a specific mechanism that aimed on the contrary to pacify it.

---

13   These were the decree on refractory priests, and the decree of the encampment of 20,000 men to defend Paris.
14   *Archives parlementaires*, vol. 45, p. 417 (20 June 1792).
15   This is indeed Hegel's expression; see *Phenomenology of Spirit*, para. 589.

THE ASSEMBLY MUST TRANSLATE THE
EMOTIONS OF THE SOVEREIGN PEOPLE

The revolutionaries were aware of the volcanic character of popular emotions. In June 1792, the question of insurrection was debated at the Jacobin club. Jean Bon Saint-André contrasted 'the insurrection of a people of slaves that is accompanied by every horror' with 'that of a free people', which was 'simply the expression subject to the general will to change or modify certain articles of the Constitution'.[16] This argument aimed to avoid attaching to the idea of insurrection 'that of revolt and carnage'.[17] A poem sent by citizen Desforges in spring 1792 is particularly eloquent in this respect:

> And in the great theatre where fate has placed us,
> liberty means life and licence death.
> Licence dares everything with no thought
> to the custom of sovereign laws or a wise liberty;
> 'free' is the word for a man, not for a raging beast.
> There are, my friends, imperious rights
> and eternal laws that must not be infringed.
> If we flouted these we would have too much to fear
> from the whole world, as history can witness.
> The first of these rights is the first need,
> ever arising anew, that each has for the other.
> Rescue my good and I shall rescue yours,
> and I shall impose on myself the respectable law
> of daring all for the man that risks all for me.
> Then you can understand how, at a moment of crisis,
> a whole people is kindled and electrified . . .[18]

---

16   Société des Jacobins, 19 June 1792. Alphonse Aulard (ed.), *La Société des Jacobins. Receuil de documents pour l'étude de la Société des Jacobins*, vol. 4, Paris: Librairie Jouaust, Librairie Noblet & Maison Quantin, 1892, p. 19.
17   Ibid.
18   Arch. Nat., série C150, L253, p. 2.

It is mutual aid, then, that gives legitimate insurrection its value, over against a generalized massacre committed by the 'furious' who are outside the laws and devoid of political value. Those who brought the word of the people to the Assembly were no less aware of this. When they demanded that the *patrie* be declared in danger, they mentioned this problem quite explicitly. In an address of the Marseillais on 19 June 1792, for example: 'Popular force makes for all your force; you have it in your grasp, use it. Too long a constraint would weaken it or lose it.'[19] And in Santerre's speech of 20 June 1792:

> The people have stood up, ready to avenge their outraged national majesty. These rigorous measures are justified by article 2 of the Rights of Man: 'Resistance to oppression'. What misfortune, however, for the free men who have handed you all your powers to see themselves reduced to drenching their hands in the blood of the conspirators!
>
> . . .
>
> Shall the people be forced to return to the time of 13 July, to themselves take up the sword of the law and avenge with one blow the outraged law, to punish the guilty and the cowardly depositaries of this very law? No, gentlemen – you see our concerns and alarms, and you will dissipate them.[20]

The means for dissipating these fears lay in giving popular enthusiasm a normative symbolic form. It was explicitly demanded that the sovereign emotive power of the people, so that it should not turn destructive, be translated into terms of law. These emotions, from pain through to rage, had therefore to be deposited by the people in the hands of the legislators, in the sacred

---

19   *Archives parlementaires*, vol. 45, p. 397.
20   Ibid., p. 417.

precincts of the Assembly, and to find their place there: 'It is in your breast that the French people deposits its alarms, and that it hopes at last to find the remedy for its ills . . . We have deposited in your breast a great pain . . .' The legislators had first of all to listen to the political pain of the people, to understand that this pain, if overcome, could produce anger, and then to re-translate this into the symbolic order so as to channel it. 'Legislators, you will not refuse the authorization of the law to those ready to go and die to defend it.'[21]

Confronted with popular emotions, therefore, the legislators, as free and sensitive men, had to become good translators of the voice of the people. And this had already found its expression, symbolized by such spokesmen as Santerre. But the intersubjectivity that was anticipated relied not on an argument to be rationally debated, but rather on a sensibility to be shared. The heart had to be touched more than the mind.

> For a long time we have comforted our ulcerated hearts. We hope that the latest cry we address to you will make your own heart feel. The people have stood up, they await in silence a response that is finally worthy of their sovereignty.[22]

The role of legislators in the process of pacification was therefore fundamental. They had to effect the translation of emotions into laws, into what a number of addresses termed the 'sanctuary of the laws', a sacred place in which men came together to make and guard laws. They thus gave a legal form to emotions, and above all invented the symbolic forms and practices that would permit enthusiasm to be contained. The spokesmen themselves invented a pacifying gesture. On 19 June, a deputation asked to be received with its

---

21   Ibid., p. 397 (19 June 1792).
22   Ibid., p. 417.

weapons, after planting a liberty tree. They then did a few dance steps in the Assembly precinct, to the sound of a drum: we can speak of a ritual of pacification. But the issues were focused in the reception of the emotions expressed in the addresses, petitions and deputations that spoke for the people. The petition of 20 June divided the Assembly: the right called the Marseillais and the faubourg Saint-Antoine 'factious', whereas the left reasserted the need to translate popular emotions into the order of the law. Lamarque:

> Coblenz says that enthusiastic patriots are factious. Gentlemen, the only true patriots are enthusiastic ones . . . I pride myself on being one of these factious. You will ask if I am referring to the petition of pikes? Yes, gentlemen. I speak of the decrees of the National Assembly; I speak of the law; I speak of the countless number of petitions that you hear each day at the tribune, and that proclaim without ambiguity the wish of the nation.[23]

To demand in June 1792 that the *patrie* be declared in danger meant demanding carnage and fury, so as to forestall the possibility of frenzy: a pacification by means of a decree that reflected quite precisely a love of the laws; the recognition of popular sovereignty, the opening of the National Guard to 'passive' citizens, and the right to legitimate violence on the part of all citizens of the male sex.[24]

Jean de Bry, a legislator of the left, in his report of 30 June 1792, replied both to the people who wanted

---

23   Ibid., p. 435 (21 June 1792).
24   Under the 1791 constitution, 'passive' citizens were those who paid less than three livres in tax, along with women and children. Putting an end to passive citizenship meant essentially ending any regime based on assets, and opening the National Guard to young people and the popular classes. Women and girls could still not join this new National Guard.

the *patrie* to be proclaimed in danger, and to the right of the Assembly that incriminated the same people for having dared to enter the king's residence on 20 June. He asserted that, if the *patrie* had to be declared in danger, it was up to the Assembly to do so in order to produce order. The nation had to be 'a well-disciplined body that, without consuming itself in useless movements, calmly awaits the order of a leader in order to act. The nation will march if need be, but it will march together and regularly.'[25] Sovereign power, therefore, was not truly settled on the side of the people, who could simply be instrumentalized when necessity demanded: 'Convinced that by reserving for itself the right to declare the danger', the Assembly 'puts off the moment and calls for calm in the minds of good citizens. The formula to utter will be: "Citizens, the *patrie* is in danger".'[26]

The same preoccupation with order can be seen with Danton on 12 August 1793: 'Let us know how to take advantage of this memorable day. You have been told that a *levée en masse* is needed. Yes, to be sure, but this must be done with order.'[27] Order so as to avoid carnage; order as a means to control the sovereign power.

But between spring 1792 and summer 1793, the hypothesis of an Assembly, supposedly representing the sovereign people but by its inaction forcing free men to 'drench their hands in the blood of conspirators', had become actual experience with the September massacres.

---

25 *Archives parlementaires*, vol. 45, p. 707.
26 Ibid.
27 *Le Moniteur universel*, vol. 17, pp. 387–8 (12 August 1793).

2

THE SEPTEMBER MASSACRES

On 30 June 1792, Delaunay, a deputy of the left, asserted that the moment had come to declare the *patrie* in danger:

> The people, cognizant of the peril to the public good, are awaiting a strong and extraordinary measure on the part of those to whom they have entrusted their destiny. They know that your mission is to carry out their wish and to legislate what is required by the nation. Maintaining the constitution can become a superstition contrary to the general national will. However immense the powers of the Constituent Assembly may be, they do not have the power of commanding the passions. I tell you, gentlemen, that so long as the state of revolution persists in an empire, a constitutional commitment can only ever signify commitment neither to add nor to subtract anything until the date set for such a revision.[1]

Not only was Delaunay's proposal not acceptable at that moment, but the Assembly proceeded towards the

---

1 Jean de Bry. *Archives parlementaires*, vol. 45, p. 707.

indictment of the men of 20 June 1792, under the
aegis of Lafayette and a petition from Le Havre of 6
July, which demanded 'vengeance on the wretches
who violated the asylum of the hereditary representative, vengeance on those factious who summoned him
with daggers in their hands'.[2] As against the king's
sacred character, associated with that of the constitution of 1791 and both allegedly profaned, the sacrality
of the people and the Declaration of the Rights of Man
and of the Citizen were now proclaimed. Could
the honour of the people be scorned in the name of the
honour of the king?

The conflict crystallized in terms of indictment:
indict the people or indict Lafayette. On 9 August
1792, the Assembly voted by a quite large majority
that it was acceptable to acquit the general, even
though he was accused of having sought to overthrow
the national representative body and had betrayed his
military mission by coming to Paris to threaten the
people. The following day, 10 August, the taking of the
Tuileries and the establishment of an insurrectionary
Commune took place without the Assembly being
forewarned or consulted: the Assembly was simply
informed of these events. Its prevarications regarding
the '*patrie* in danger', and its ambiguous attitude
towards Lafayette, radically brought into question the
trust that the people had granted it. No longer was it a
matter of awaiting the signal of the law in order to
insubordinately rise and demand the abdication of the
perjured king. Contrary to what had occurred on 20
June, there was no longer any sense in waiting for a
decree before acting. The decree would not come in
time. The Assembly was no longer a possible site for
the sacred translation of the will of the people, but
simply a place for registering accomplished facts. In

---

2   Petition from Le Havre. *Archives parlementaires*, vol. 46, p. 163 (6
July 1792).

September 1792, a new step was taken in this disavowal of the Assembly. This was because the Parisians'
dread no longer arose simply from the defeats suffered
on the French borders, but also from the sense of being
betrayed by legislators who had not taken the measures called for by the insurrection of 10 August, and in
particular by those measures aimed at 'judging the
crimes of 10 August'.

When the Swiss Guards opened fire, the Marseilles
fédérés, the Paris sans-culottes and the National Guards
were already engaged in the Tuileries. They came
armed, aware that the king and the royal family had
been put under protection, and desired that in this context there should be no spilling of blood. They
undoubtedly remembered that 'the insurrection of a
free people is the expression, arising from the general
will, to change the Constitution', and that it presupposes the self-control of violence. If they came armed,
this was to express the effective shift in the sovereign
power, the change of the constitution *in fact*. They had
come ready to fight to take the Tuileries as they had
taken the Bastille. But the palace did not appear to
resist their entry, which was made in calm. If justice
was demanded for the crimes of 10 August, this was
with the feeling of having been caught in an ambush
aiming to spill the blood of the people, when the political die was already cast. It was because they sensed the
betrayal of what should be a *common* desire, bound up
with the *common* sense of natural humanity not to
spill blood, that the Parisians of 10 August demanded
justice. If there was intolerable cruelty, this was on the
part of the defenders of the palace. To deal with and
pacify the emotions that arose in the face of such treason, justice needed to be promptly done. This demand
for justice was also a way of restoring trust in the
Assembly, while waiting for the meeting of the National
Convention promised for September. No one wished
to spend too long on pacifying symbolic mediations,

and only the renewal of these mediations could prove that popular sovereignty had been genuinely established, that citizens were now recognized as equal, fully disposing of the sovereign power. If justice was done, the insurrection would then have truly established democratic principles without dislocating the community of citizens. If justice was refused, this would be the sign of an uncertain, fragile and thwarted foundation. The political community would then be torn apart, and the insurrectionary confrontation renewed in forms that would certainly be more difficult to control: not the forms of a velvet insurrection, but those of the public vengeance of the people. This was a matter of importance, and Robespierre, Danton and Marat all stressed the necessity of a tribunal that would judge these crimes. Robespierre intervened on 15 August, as a delegate of the Commune, and proclaimed: 'Since 10 August, the just vengeance of the people has not yet been satisfied.'[3] On the 17th, a citizen and temporary representative of the Commune declared at the tribune of the Assembly:

> As citizen, as magistrate of the people, I come to announce to you that tonight at midnight the tocsin will sound, the call to arms will be given. The people are tired of not being at all avenged. You should fear lest they make their own justice. I demand that you decree without hesitation the appointment of a citizen in each section to form a criminal tribunal.[4]

The deputies Choudieu and Thuriot sought to challenge this representative's legitimacy by maintaining that he did not know the 'true principles and true laws'. In the event, the Assembly did not proclaim the decree

---

3   Robespierre. *Archives parlementaires*, vol. 48, p. 180 (15 August 1792).
4   *Le Moniteur universel*, vol. 13, p. 443 (17 August 1792).

demanded, while the tribunal established on 17 August, far from adopting this extraordinary form of popular tribunal, simply renewed the regular legal forms. The September massacres thus found the deputies marginalized, one could say 'absent', i.e. their presence no longer counted for the protagonists of the event. When representatives of the constituted authorities – whether those of the Assembly, the departmental directory or the municipality – appeared before the Septembrists using the language of the law, this language was no longer effective. Their speech had become unwelcome. Reference to the law had lost its sacred character.

The emotional economy I have described, which is also that of the sacred, had thus broken down. The sacred voice of the people demanding vengeance – 'vox populi, vox dei'[5] – had not been listened to or translated into law by those whose function this was. The representatives had lost their position as necessary intercessors. From now on, the people expected nothing more from the Assembly, and the acts of the Septembrists would make a gap between this de facto delegitimized representation and the people. Reference to the law was no longer a demand from the people but an imposition by their representatives, whose legitimacy to proclaim the law or 'make it speak'[6] had been invalidated. In practice, then, they were no longer recognized as representatives. The transaction between sacred text and sacred body could no longer find expression, and a relation of body to body was now substituted for the symbolic operation that had become impossible.

In the written records of representatives of the constituted authorities, the insurgents' absence of animosity

---

5 For an analysis of this expression see Michel Poizat, *Vox populi, vox dei. La voix en politique*, Paris: Métaillié, 2000.
6 According to the recorded expression, as Jacques Guilhaumou has shown in *La langue politique et la Révolution française*, Paris: Méridiens Klincksieck, 1989.

towards them is striking. For example, when Pétion appeared at the prison of La Force, he was neither turned away nor molested. We even get the impression that the Parisians would have liked to be able to please him by obeying his instructions, but that their duty had changed:

> I spoke to them in the austere language of the law, I spoke with the sentiment of deep indignation that I felt. I made them all come out before me. But I had hardly appeared myself before they went back inside.[7]

This disavowal does not indicate the expression of a new aggressiveness, but rather that intermediaries who had not managed to elaborate the laws indispensable for public safety were declared useless and negligible. Nonetheless, certain arguments still resonated:

> When the mayor of Versailles requested pardon for the innocent, Blomquel, one of the protagonists of the events who was directing operations, replied by making them come out. The mayor, however, was unable to distinguish between the innocent and the guilty.[8]

What was involved in the September massacres, then, was not an indifferent, disproportionate and blind vengeance, opposed all along the line to criminal justice. Nor was this vengeance a desire that the law could restrain. Far from being the expression of a vindictive passion, the vengeance carried out appears above all as the exercise of a difficult charge that was forced on people by duty. One of the difficulties in executing it

7 *Le Moniteur universel*, vol. 14, p. 428.
8 According to the charge sheet of 20 Vendémaire year III (AD Seine et Oise, 42 L 58), cited by Bernard Conein, *Langage politique et mode d'affrontement. Le jacobinisme et les massacres de Septembre*, PhD thesis, Paris: EHESS, 1978.

was precisely to distinguish the innocent from the guilty, to trace this dividing line – a question that constantly appears in the major reports of the period of Terror. Robespierre put it like this on 5 Nivôse of year II:

> And so, if we regarded as criminals all those who, in the revolutionary movement, exceeded the precise line drawn by prudence, we would encompass in a common proscription along with bad citizens, all the natural friends of liberty, your own friends and all the supports of the Republic . . . What can then untangle all these distinctions? What can draw the dividing line between all the contrary excesses? Love of the *patrie* and of truth.[9]

Vengeance maintains the distinction between social groups and constructs their respective identities – here that of the sovereign people towards those who refuse them this sovereignty or do not respect it, those who are responsible for the denial of justice and the guilty who remain unpunished. If the order of *penalty* assumes that offender and offended belong to one and the same group, the order of *vengeance* 'is inscribed in an intermediary social space between that in which the proximity of partners prohibits it and that in which their distance substitutes war for vengeance'.[10] An approach of this kind undermines a supposed evolutionary opposition between vengeance and justice: vengeance is not a more archaic form of justice than penal justice, but a form of justice corresponding to a different social configuration. It is more a question of understanding vengeance as a moment of constitutive justice of the specific identity of each of the social groups that confront one another within the same society. It is at one and the same time

---

9 Robespierre, *Pour le Bonheur et pour la Liberté*, p. 277.
10 Raymond Verdier (ed.), *La vengeance. Études d'ethnologie, d'histoire et de philosophie*, vol. 1, Paris: Éditions Cujas, 1980, p. 24.

> a system of exchange and social control of violence . . .
> As an integral part of the overall social system, the
> system of retribution is above all an ethic that deploys
> an ensemble of representations and values relating to
> life and death, to time and space . . . it is finally an
> instrument and site of power identifying and opposing
> social units and vindicatory groups.[11]

This long definition casts a new light on the revolutionary call for vengeance. It shows how, far from being
disqualifying, this exhortation appeals to an ethic in
which the disturbing question of duty appears. The
demand for vengeance implies a reaction designed to
obtain respect for the identity of the victim's group:

> In this sense, the debt of the offence can be defined as
> a debt of life, and life as a spiritual and social capital
> that the members of the group are charged with
> defending and making fruitful . . . This life-capital is
> depicted by two symbols: blood, symbol of the union
> and continuity of generations, and honour, symbol
> of the identity and difference that makes it possible
> both to recognize the other and to demand that he
> respects you.[12]

When the spokesmen of the people called for vengeance for the crimes of 10 August, the 'debt of life'
was that of the blood of the patriots, but also that of
the honour of the people whose identity as conquering
people was challenged. In revolutionary terms, re-
establishing honour amounted to manifesting the
identity of the sovereign people irrevocably by an act
of vengeance. This is why the public vengeance
demanded was not an a priori vengeance,[13] not a pre-

---

11   Ibid., p. 16.
12   Ibid., p. 19.
13   As against the standpoint initially developed by Jules Michelet, and

ventive vengeance carried out by patriots before leaving for the battlefront, but rather a subsequent vengeance for an affront that was hard to repair.

A SOVEREIGN VENGEANCE

In the *Créole patriote* for 2 September, the account begins by evoking 10 August: 'The people, justly indignant at the crimes committed during the *journée* of 10 August, made for the prisons. They still feared plots and traitors . . . The news that Verdun had been taken . . . provoked their resentment and vengeance.'[14] On 6 September, Mlle de Mareuil, daughter of a member of the Commune's general council, wrote to her brother:

> I have to make the following remark: since the *journée* of 10 August, there have only been three people guillotined, and this has revolted the people. Finally people gathered from all sides . . . Oh my dear friend, we are all in a state of dreadful consternation.[15]

The same day, *La Sentinelle* expressed very clearly how 'the crowd, weary at the silence of the laws, delivered swift justice'.[16] On 11 September, the tribunal of 17 August itself sent an address to the Assembly:

> The slow pace of the forms [of justice], healthy and just in time of calm, was deadly at a time when the prisons themselves had become centres of conspiracy and workshops of revolt, in which criminals already

---

reprised under this concept of 'a priori vengeance' by Antoine de Baecque, *La gloire et l'effroi. Sept morts sous la terreur*, Paris: Grasset, 1997, p. 86.

14   Cited after Pierre Caron, *Les Massacres de Septembre*, Paris, 1935.
15   Ibid., p. 131.
16   Ibid., p. 132.

judged by their country were planning a deadly explosion. The national crowd struck the parricides; the people and heaven were avenged.[17]

This failure on the part of the legal institutions in the face of treason and unpunished crimes led to a foundation which was deprived of symbolic mediation. From 2 to 6 September, the sovereign power identified itself with a 'making die' that fused the various powers – legislative, executive and judicial – in a single movement.[18] But those who killed were presented in the immediate commentaries as victims, as people who deserved sympathy. Thus Mme Julien from the Drôme, the partner of the deputy: 'My friend, I cast a veil here with a trembling hand over the crimes that the people were forced to commit by all those whose sorry victim they have been for three years.'[19] In the *Chronique de Paris* for 4th September, we can read: 'The spilling of blood caused a wretched sensation . . . It is an unfortunate and terrible situation when the character of a people naturally good and generous is forced to deliver itself to such acts of vengeance.'[20] Finally, *Le Moniteur* of the same date spoke of

events that any decent man would wish to cover with a veil and withdraw from history. But the counter-revolutionaries are indeed far more guilty than [are]

---

17 Cited after Caron, *Les Massacres de Septembre*, p. 132.
18 According to Pierre Serna, there cannot be just the exercise of executive power, even an 'executive power of execution'. Serna maintains that 'the representatives were afraid of popular violence. The executive power of execution, if this expression is permissible, was seized by the population of Paris, and demanded that the men of Versailles should restore public order'; in Joël Cornette (ed.), *La monarchie entre renaissance et révolution, 1515–1792*, Paris: Seuil, 2000, p. 400. When the three powers are fused, the notion of executive power is no longer apposite; what we have here is indeed a sovereign power, in this case that of popular sovereignty.
19 Cited after Caron, *Les Massacres de Septembre*, p. 124.
20 Ibid., p. 127.

certain illegal avengers of their crimes. Humanity is in
no wise consoled, but the mind is left less disturbed.[21]

The scene of the September massacres could be inter-
preted as the sovereign scene described both by Walter
Benjamin and Giorgio Agamben. In his *Critique of
Violence*, Benjamin maintained that

> all mythic, lawmaking violence, which we may call 'exec-
> utive', is pernicious. Pernicious, too, is the law-preserving,
> 'administrative' violence that serves it. Divine violence,
> which is the sign and seal but never the means of sacred
> dispatch, may be called 'sovereign' violence.[22]

This 'divine violence' is the violence of *vox populi, vox
dei*. To recognize the divine character of this violence,
as of this voice, does not mean drawing support from
established religion to legitimize a violence which is
underway or a voice that takes bodily form. It is rather
to maintain that the blood spilled is not that of mythical sacrifice – which, according to Benjamin, 'demands
it for its own sake against pure and simple life' – but
rather that of a *divine violence* that 'accepts sacrifice
for the sake of the living'. This is why

> those who base a condemnation of all violent killing of
> one person by another on the commandment ['Thou
> shalt not kill'] are therefore mistaken. It exists not as a
> criterion of judgment, but as a guideline for the actions
> of persons or communities who have to wrestle with it
> in solitude and, in exceptional cases, to take on them-
> selves the responsibility of ignoring it.[23]

---

21 *Le Moniteur universel*, vol. 14.
22 Walter Benjamin, 'Critique of Violence', trans. E. Jephcott, in
Selected Writings, vol. 1: 1913–26, ed. M. Bullock and M. W. Jennings,
Cambridge, MA: Belknap Press, 1996, p. 86.
23 Ibid., p. 87.

This solitude of decision is that of the sovereign power. For Giorgio Agamben, 'the sovereign sphere is the sphere in which it is permitted to kill without committing homicide and without celebrating a sacrifice'; as for the lives of those massacred, they are the 'sacred lives' of homo sacer, exposed to murder and unsacrificable, captured in the 'first properly political space of the West distinct from both the religious and the profane sphere, from both the natural order and the regular juridical order'.[24] These theoretical illuminations help us understand how everyone has found the September massacres intolerable, despite the great majority of spectators finding them legitimate at the time.

The commentaries of radical revolutionaries on the September massacres use the notions of justice and vengeance indifferently – a proof that the lapse of ordinary institutions leads to the vengeance of the laws, or of the people, since for the revolutionaries avenging the people meant avenging the laws. These commentators insist on the necessity of recognizing that it was indeed the people that acted. For Marat: 'The people have the right to take up the sword of justice when the judges are concerned only to protect the guilty and oppress the innocent.'[25] Such statements find their place in registering the failure of legal institutions, the National Assembly and the tribunals, which no longer championed the respect due to the people as a group. Robespierre spoke of 'the justice of the people thus expiated, by the punishment of several counter-revolutionary aristocrats who dishonoured the French name, the eternal impunity of all the oppressors of humanity'.[26] The people, a social group inscribed in the *longue durée* of history as against the social group of the

---

24 Agamben, *Homo Sacer*, pp. 83-4.
25 *Journal de la République française*, 25 October 1792.
26 *Le Défenseur de la Constitution*, 20 September 1792.

'oppressors of humanity', defended the honour of its name. On 13 Ventôse of year II (3 March 1794), before maintaining that happiness was a new idea in Europe, Saint-Just encouraged the people to preserve this honour: 'Make yourselves respected by pronouncing with pride the destiny of the French people. Avenge the people for twelve hundred years of offences against their fathers.'[27] On 26 Germinal of year II (16 April 1794), he accused history of 'several centuries of folly' as against 'five years of resistance to oppression', emphasizing the values borne by the name of Frenchman as the name of the people in the revolutionary project. 'What is a king as opposed to a Frenchman?' The name of Frenchman made it possible both to say what was to come, and to define the present conflictual division between oppressors and oppressed. It was on this basis that the name of the people was really constituted. In his reply to Jean-Baptiste Louvet, who accused him in November 1792 of having failed to prevent the massacres and perhaps even having encouraged them, Robespierre could argue that it was necessary to read in the September massacres an act of popular sovereignty:

> Can magistrates stop the people? It was indeed a popular movement, not the partial sedition of a few wretches to murder their kind . . . What could magistrates do against the determined will of an indignant people, who opposed to their speeches both the memory of a victory won over tyranny and the devotion with which they were about to hurl themselves against the Prussians, and who reproached the very laws for the long impunity of the traitors who tore the breast of their *patrie*?[28]

---

27 Saint-Just, *Œuvres complètes*, p. 714.
28 National Convention, 5 November 1792, in reply to the accusation of Jean-Baptiste Louvet. *Archives parlementaires*, vol. 52, p. 162.

The appropriation of sovereignty by the people did not in the end indicate a transfer of sacrality, but rather the application of a sacrality, a mode of action specific to the political. '"Sacred insurrection", "sacred duty" were commonplace phrases in the language of the sections in August 1792 and May 1793', and this vengeance was likewise defined as sacred by a number of patriots: 'National vengeance is every bit as just, as sacred, and perhaps more indispensable than insurrection itself.'[29]

It is possible to regret that the foundation of sovereign power should rest on the exercise of the sovereign exception, just as it is to deplore that the representatives of the people refused to translate the voice of the people and thus brought them to this replay of sovereign foundation, to vengeance effected without symbolic mediation. As early as 20 June 1792, the popular spokesmen feared a breach in the sacred bonds of law that united the people with the Assembly. Santerre reminded the representatives of the people that they had 'sworn before heaven not to abandon our cause [i.e. the cause of popular sovereignty], to die to defend it', and addressed them in the following terms: 'Remember, gentlemen, this sacred oath, and suffer the people, afflicted in their turn, not to ask if you have abandoned them.'[30]

Despite this defection, the Septembrists founded popular sovereignty in an irreversible manner, by assuming the sovereign exception as popular vengeance. Those who maintain that there was no crime, but rather an exercise of sovereignty, are faithful to this way of seeing things: like the Septembrists, they take a political decision on which they refuse to concede. This was true at the moment of the trial of the

29   Cited from Lucas, 'Revolutionary Violence, the People and the Terror', pp. 69, 73.
30   *Archives parlementaires*, vol. 45, p. 417 (20 June 1792).

king, when what was at issue was not only the fate to be meted out to the royal traitor, but also and indissociably, the reinterpretation of 10 August 1792 and the September massacres. It was true again in the *journées* of 31 May to 2 June 1793, with the exclusion of those representatives who refused to understand what they had witnessed on 20 June, 10 August and 2–3 September 1792 – namely, the founding appropriation of popular sovereignty. A triad of events in 1792 and a series of interpretations of these events in 1793 thus led up to the same decision, that of founding popular sovereignty by assuming what was then called the Terror – or said differently, the employment of sovereign vengeance by the people.

THE SENTIMENTS OF NATURAL HUMANITY
AND POLITICAL HUMANITY

How could the agents of a public vengeance that led to the spilling of blood claim the sentiment of humanity? Those revolutionaries who refused to incriminate the Septembrists maintained that a human society, full of humanity, had to envisage not only the principle of sovereign exception, but also the necessity of transforming that principle into action. A democratic republic had to succeed in holding the sovereign exception to the margins of political life, had to manage to avoid spilling blood by way of the power of symbolic mediations suited to translating the voice of the people into political *logos*. The sentiment of humanity dictated a greater responsibility on the part of the representatives, who had to assume violence so as not to let it thoughtlessly spread. The September massacres, insufferable but justifiable, paradoxically offer an initial angle of analysis for understanding the revolutionary use of the notion of 'humanity' and the sentiment of humanity.

Replying to Jean-Baptiste Louvet, Robespierre, while acknowledging the value of a sentiment of natural humanity, maintained that, in a context of avenging the laws, no one could allow themselves to lament what happened to the body of the enemy. Robespierre thereby redrew the camp of friends to be avenged, against the lack of differentiation produced by the sentiment of natural humanity and a concern for all victims outside any political consideration. Paraphrasing the *Marseillaise*, he pleaded for a sentiment of revolutionary humanity:

> Weep for the guilty victims assigned to the revenge of the laws, who fell under the sword of popular justice; but let your grief have an end, as with all human things. Keep some tears for more touching calamities. Weep for a hundred thousand patriots slain by tyranny, weep for our citizens dying under the fires of their roofs, and the sons of citizens murdered in the cradle or in the arms of their mothers. Do you not also have brothers, children and wives to avenge? The family of French legislators is the *patrie*; it is the entire human race apart from tyrants and their accomplices. Weep then for humanity dead under their hateful yoke. But console yourselves if, imposing silence on all common passions, you wish to ensure the happiness of your country and prepare that of the world, console yourselves if you wish to restore exiled equality and justice on earth, and to uproot by just laws the source of crimes and the misfortunes of your kind. A sensitivity that trembles almost exclusively for the enemies of liberty strikes me as suspect.[31]

Robespierre is thus replying here with a veritable call to vengeance, and stressing the necessity to choose one's camp in order to found the values of the Revolution: happiness, equality, justice. For, if

31   Robespierre. *Archives parlementaires*, vol. 3, p. 62 (28 September 1792).

the institution of vengeance avoids the blind unleash-
ing of violence and establishes socially founding
moral values ... once it exists, it demands that its
members make crucial choices, towards both the
living and the dead, that they make a commitment
towards these values.[32]

The pain at having witnessed massacres – which did
indeed wound the sensibility of the time, marked as
this was by the desire to no longer make the human
body the place where the symbolic register was
expressed – had to have an 'end', in Robespierre's
expression. Despite the deep pain caused by the effects
of avenging the laws, he summoned revolutionaries to
choose their camp: the sentiment of political humanity,
which was also the exercise of sovereign judgement for
the citizenry as a whole, had to prevail in each person
over the sentiment of natural humanity. And it was this
political sentiment that established the boundary
between friends and enemies, making perceptible and
explicit the question of vengeance.

The revolutionaries directly experienced this conflict
over human sentiments, and the manner in which they
dealt with it determined their political camp. On 28
December, speaking about the king, Robespierre
described this conflict with the greatest of clarity:

I felt republican virtue vacillate in my heart on seeing
this guilty man humiliated before the sovereign
power ... I could even add that I share with the weakest among us all the particular emotions that can
interest us in the fate of the accused ... Both hatred of
tyrants and love of humanity have a common source in
the heart of the just man. Citizens, the ultimate test of
devotion that representatives owe to their *patrie* is to

32 D. Vidal, 'Vengeance', in *Dictionnaire de l'ethnologie et de
l'anthropologie*, p. 738.

strangle these initial movements of natural sensitivity
in favour of the safety of a great people and of
oppressed humanity! Citizens, the sensitivity that sac-
rifices innocence to crime is a cruel sensitivity, the
mercy that compromises with tyranny is barbaric.[33]

To which Sèze replied: 'Frenchmen, the revolution that
regenerates you has developed in you great virtues, but
beware that it has not weakened in your souls the sentiment of humanity, without which there can only be
wrongdoing.'[34]

It was thus in the name of humanity, and to struggle
against one's particular emotions, that it became
imperative in the eyes of the revolutionaries to constrain their immediate sentiment of humanity. In year
II, this conflict was again apparent when political
hatred of the English government's accomplice[35] had
to be asserted:

> As a Frenchman, a representative of the people, I
> declare that I hate the English people . . . I am inter-
> ested in the English only as a man; I admit, then, that I
> feel some pain at seeing so great a number subject to
> scoundrels . . . This pain in me is so great that I confess
> it is from hatred of its government that I have drawn
> the hatred I bear to this people.[36]

The Terror thus brought two sentiments of humanity
into conflict. One of these, committed to saving bodies
indifferently (those of friends, enemies, accomplices,

---

33   Robespierre. *Archives parlementaires*, vol. 56, p. 16 (28 December
1792).

34   Albert Soboul, *Le procès de Louis XVI*, Paris: Archives Juillard,
1966, pp. 139, 148.

35   I have drawn here from my *L'Impossible citoyen. L'étranger dans
le discours de la révolution française*, Paris: Albin Michel, 1997; and
especially from the third section, 'Fraternité et exclusion'.

36   A. Aulard, *La société des Jacobins*, vol. 5, p. 633.

traitors, slaves) so as not to injure its sentiment of natural humanity, was attached above all to the life of each human being *as such*, while the other was attached to preserving the meaning that a person wishes to give to life, to the common wellbeing. Emotion towards living human beings seems constrained by a different emotion, arising from the risk of seeing damage not to human bodies, not to bare lives, but to the foundation of their humanity, i.e. their mutual liberty.

This is why 'we have to desire the Terror as we desire liberty'.[37] This is always an effort – a constraint on oneself, on one's personal sentiments, on natural emotions. Here, what is involved with the definition of the sentiment of 'humanity' as no longer a natural but a political sentiment is also the notion of 'fraternity', which must no longer describe the vast family of the human race, but rather the political capacity of men to produce effective conventions of peace. In this respect, 'fraternity' becomes above all else a political sentiment specific to men who respect natural right. The notion of 'humanity' is then no longer a descriptive notion, but a prescriptive one: it is the dutiful character of the human race, provided that the French revolutionaries do not fail.

It is in this context that the notion of sensibility replaces that of raw emotion. In fact, if it is agreed that emotions derange, it is expected of the revolutionary that he should forge his new sensibility as a free man in the thick of events, and respond in this way to the prescriptive character of humanity. The emotion experienced in a particular situation thus makes it possible to politically judge the quality of the man of revolution. Robespierre's accusation against Camille Desmoulins and *Le Vieux Cordelier* is exemplary in this respect. While in 1789 the sensitive man, and more

---

37 Claude Lefort, 'La Terreur révolutionnaire', *Passé/Présent* 2 (1983), p. 25.

particularly the sensitive lawyer, was politically opposed to the perverted aristocracy,[38] in 1793 and 1794 a division of sensibility took place within a sensitive common humanity, and increasingly explicitly referred to what we still today call 'political sensibilities'. The plurality of political sensibilities during the Terror thus meant a plurality of politics of terror. What Camille Desmoulins proposed was not to renounce terror towards the Girondins ('I have never spoken for a clemency of moderation, clemency for the leaders'),[39] but rather to conceive of it differently. For him, terror was indeed a response to the risk of an overflow of punitive emotions, and in this respect it was actually conceived as a procedure of pacification towards the intolerable. But this procedure can go into reverse if the boundary between bad men and men of goodwill – those with a just reputation for having a heart – is impossible to draw. What clemency proposes is a particular line for this boundary, a boundary that claims to properly restore civil trust. By admitting that man is always a fallible and divided being ('Since when is man infallible and exempt from error?'),[40] Desmoulins claimed that political action should not aim to distinguish between good and bad but rather between those who had gone astray and those who were irredeemable. The *Comité de clémence* should therefore recognize the irredeemable, and help those who vacillated not to collapse into counter-revolution. This impossible boundary had to be worked on within each individual. Whereas terror sought to produce a system of external constrains, Desmoulins proposed a policy aiming to lead the subject to freedom. His conception of truth was radically opposed to that of Robespierre. If both agreed in basing truth on the *forum interior*, for

---

38   Sarah Maza, *Vies privées, affaires publiques*, Paris: Fayard, 1997.
39   *Le Vieux Cordelier*, Paris: Belin, 1989, p. 90.
40   Ibid., p. 75.

Robespierre that truth was either whole or nil: any fault destroyed the subject totally. For Desmoulins, on the contrary, truth remained relative or polemical. Referring to Galileo and his '*eppur si muove*', he argued that truth and error were not absolutes but figures of convention. It was thus in the name of an extremely modern conception of truth that Desmoulins proposed to base his *Comité de clémence*, without abandoning the quest for a universal republican truth. Desmoulins introduced the plurality of political sensibilities – from the very fact of political work, and his experience of the world – as a plurality of conventions that were not all equivalent, but were nevertheless all capable of evolution, transformation and displacement. Robespierre rather hoped for a radical change in political sensibility on the part of his contemporaries. This did not come about, and republicans could only grow melancholy in tracking down their ever more numerous enemies. Camille Desmoulins hoped to rescue the greater part of anachronistic sensibilities. The abyss of terror swallowed them up, rendering impossible such a work of political conflict as a conflict of sensibilities. After Thermidor, politics would no longer be the place of a division of sensibilities; it rather became the place of professional distribution of knowledge of the social art.[41]

---

41 This expression, coined by the Physiocrats, was commonly used by Sieyès, and is analyzed by Jacques Guilhaumou in *Sieyès et l'ordre de la langue? L'invention de la politique moderne*, Paris: Kimé, 2002.

3

THE TERROR AS A LONG CYCLE OF VENGEANCE: TOWARDS A REINTERPRETATION OF THE LAWS OF TERROR

The establishment of the revolutionary tribunal on 9 March 1793, the law of suspects of 17 September 1793, and the reorganization of this extraordinary tribunal on 22 Prairial of year II – a reorganization which historians mark as the start of the Great Terror – are three key moments in the history of the terror, as well as of its representation. The tribunal was established before the spokesmen of September 1793 demanded that it be placed on the agenda, leading among other things to the law of suspects. This tribunal amounted to an institutional foundation and precursor of the Terror, which – for those who like a precise periodization[1] – extended from 5 September 1793 to 9 Thermidor of year II. It was perceived as a genuine break, which led certain members of the Convention to reject it violently. The tribunal, however, came into being in order to avoid a repetition of the September massacres, and was presented in this respect as a negative replay of those events. It proposed a version of violent insurrection that was channelled into a juridical apparatus, designed to avoid the people having to experience once more the scourge of non-symbolized

---

1 On the question of a periodization of the Terror, see Bronislaw Baczko, 'The Terror Before the Terror'.

vengeance: the tribunal opened a cycle of institutional vengeance. It did not break with vengeance; its logic was always one of bipolar social confrontation between people and counter-revolutionaries. It was the tribunal of vengeance.

The law of suspects is both more familiar and harder to understand. It has led historians to conceive revolutionary repression as something unlimited. Generalized suspicion provoking a runaway terror with no possible end led to the Thermidorian representation of a solitary Robespierre among a forest of guillotines. According to the impressive list of supposedly 'suspect' categories, anyone could in fact become a suspect. The representation of a revolution in which no one remained safe from a dynamic of deadly political exclusion is based on an analysis of this law, which was disturbing for the revolutionaries themselves, who feared from the start its devastating effects. In this cycle of vengeance, however, 'rules and rituals were conceived in order to open, suspend and hem in vengeance'.[2] The position I shall defend here is that this law of suspects, far from increasing deadly repression, actually suspended it. For being suspected did not amount to being accused, and if the death penalty was there potentially, it was deferred, sometimes indefinitely. By giving form to the confrontation of opposing political groups, suspicion was a response to a multiform demand for vengeance (one that is undoubtedly hard to grasp) without meting out death to the members of the offending social group. This law was a manner of deploying vengeance with a maximum scope, yet without transforming it into a generalized bloodbath. The prisons filled, but the guillotine was used relatively little in terms of the number of suspects.

But everything changed again with the tribunal of Prairial, which always leaves historians of the French

---

2   Verdier, *La vengeance*, p. 16.

Revolution speechless. While the dangers and dread that the country experienced had been removed by the end of the factional crisis and the military victories of spring 1794, this drastic reorganization of the revolutionary tribunal meant that it could only pronounce two sentences: acquittal or death. The vengeance carried out by the law of suspects chose not to make die: it was a question of 'restoring the balance between groups and thus putting an end to the cycle of vengeance'.[3] The law of Prairial took the paradoxical form of a 'making die': it was aimed no longer at a social group to be controlled, but rather at irreconcilable enemies. I shall seek to break through the totally enigmatic character of this law, by taking seriously its return to a 'making die' which this time was more akin to warfare than to penal justice or vengeance. In this sense, I believe that this law was one of the forms chosen by the revolutionaries to emerge from vengeance before they could in the end dispense with terror.

'LET US BE TERRIBLE, TO SAVE THE PEOPLE FROM BEING SO'

The revolutionary tribunal – called an 'exceptional' tribunal by historians and an 'extraordinary' tribunal by the revolutionaries themselves – was both a symbol of the Terror and a replay of the scenario of the September massacres. Its creation proceeded from a popular demand by the Paris sections, on 9 March 1793, in a context of crisis: the victorious enemy was preparing to invade the country; traitors and counter-revolutionaries remained unpunished and rose up against the republic in the Vendée, in Paris itself, as well as in the central departments; the price of bread made for a dramatic situation, and riots proliferated.

---

3   Ibid.

In that month of March 1793, the Convention member Bentabole, returning together with Tallien from a visit to the section of l'Oratoire with the aim of accelerating the *levée en masse*,

> observed that the only reason citizens were unwilling to go off was because they could see that there is no real justice in the Republic, and held that traitors and conspirators must be punished. As a consequence, they demanded a tribunal that they could be sure of, a revolutionary tribunal.[4]

Jean Bon Saint-André and Jacques-Louis David returned from the Louvre section and reported the same demand from its members:

> They begged the National Convention to punish and annihilate the plotters, so as to do *justice to the people* if the people are being deceived or badly served. They demanded . . . that the *blood* of our soldiers, spilled either by treason or by incompetence or by cowardice, be *avenged*.

The assembled members of the Louvre section had

> decreed that it invited citizens Saint-André and David, in the most pressing fashion and in the name of the *patrie*, to express its wish to the National Convention that a tribunal without appeal be immediately established, to put an end to the boldness of the major culprits and of all enemies of the public cause.[5]

At the heart of this argument lay the sacred transaction between the body of patriots and the advent of the

---

4   Bentabole, *Archives parlementaires*, vol. 60, p. 2.
5   Jean Bon Saint-André and Jacques-Louis David. *Archives parlementaires*, vol. 60, p. 3.

Republic. To spill one's blood for the *patrie* was premised on the advent of the Republic. To give the people justice within the Republic meant the justice of blood spilled on the frontiers. Vengeance and justice were indications of enthusiasm and sources of life; disgust had to be overcome, as dread had had to be overcome in 1792. Both of these mortifying emotions could lead to the annihilation of the people and the Revolution. Disgust had to be transmuted into the patriotic enthusiasm which was needed to save the Republic. As in the spring of 1792, public safety involved a transmutation of emotions. But while these had previously been bound up with the dynamic of insurrection (dread, anger, indignation), they re-emerged in March 1793 from a dynamic of aftershock. To displace dread, revolutionary anger had to be discovered and brought to insurrection. To displace disgust, this insurrection, the September massacres and the king's trial had to be followed by a genuine transformation imprinted in everyday political practices. Justice and vengeance would be its tokens. This is why only the sentiment of justice could overcome discouragement. Then it would be possible once again for people to make their bodies a rampart for liberty. We should not forget that in the revolutionary discourse it was the heart and not just the mind or reason that guaranteed the defence of the project. 'Honour the mind, but base yourselves on the heart.'[6]

On 10 March 1793, the Convention was on the point of dispersing without having established this tribunal, when Danton took the floor:

> What, citizens, can you leave without taking the great measures that public safety demand? I feel it is of utmost importance to take judicial measures that will

6 Saint-Just, 26 Germinal year II. *Archives parlementaires*, vol. 88, p. 615.

punish the counter-revolutionaries, as it is for them
that this tribunal must supplement the tribunal of popular vengeance ... If it is so hard to convict for a
political crime, is it not necessary that extraordinary
laws, taken outside of the social body, should make
rebels tremble and convict the guilty? Here public
safety demands great means and terrible measures. I
see no middle way between the ordinary forms and an
extraordinary tribunal.[7]

Danton thus presented the revolutionary tribunal as an
antidote to 'popular vengeance', or more precisely as a
potential control on this by an institution arising from
'exceptional laws, taken outside of the social body', in
this foundational sphere of popular sovereignty by sovereign vengeance. But popular vengeance re-opened
the question of the September massacres, which Buzot
had in mind when he declared that the revolutionary
tribunal would lead 'to a despotism more dreadful
than that of anarchy',[8] or when Amar recalled: 'There
is no other measure that can save the people, otherwise
it will have to rise up and fell its enemies.'[9] As for
Danton himself, he saw the revolutionary tribunal not
only as a way of putting limits to the sovereign exception in its function of vengeance, but also as an
opportunity to renew the pacifying function of the
National Assembly:

> Since some have ventured in this Assembly to recall the
> bloody days when any good citizen trembled, I will
> say, for myself, that if a tribunal had then existed, the
> people, who have been so cruelly reproached for these
> *journées*, would not have covered them with blood; I
> will say, and I have the assent of all who were witness

7   *Archives parlementaires*, vol. 60, p. 62.
8   Ibid, p. 59.
9   Ibid, p. 61.

to these events, that no human power was in a position to stem the outpouring of national vengeance. Let us profit from the mistakes of our predecessors. Let us do what the Legislative Assembly failed to do, let us be terrible so as to save the people from being so. Let us organize a tribunal – not well, for that is impossible, but as best we can, so that the sword of the law weighs over the heads of all its enemies . . . [and] so that all will be avenged.[10]

Classically, 'in the institution of vengeance, it falls to those who embody the social group as a totality to assure the mediation between protagonists and to restore, as far as possible, the state of peace'.[11] In the system of the Revolution, this function of a mediating third party between mutually confronting social groups fell first and foremost to the Assembly, which had to make laws adequate to the popular emotions, a ritualized and pacifying symbolic discourse to prevent any spillage outside of the political.[12]

Terror then appeared as a return to the translatability of popular emotions that had characterized the spring of 1792, and to the sacrality of the law; a return to the possibility of the representatives of the people finding appropriate and performative speech. Terror

---

10   Ibid, p. 62.

11   Vidal, 'Vengeance', p. 738.

12   I have used here the distinction proposed by Paolo Viola between political violence and irrational violence, which maintains that the points of extreme violence in a revolution are those 'of an irrational, not a political violence, which the revolution does not require, which are not beneficial to it, which it is horrified by, which it ends up repressing as far as possible, but which it has itself triggered because it has touched the unconscious and fragile equilibriums that govern the relationship to the sacred'. See Paolo Viola, 'Violence révolutionnaire ou violence du peuple en révolution', *Recherches sur la Révolution*, Paris: La Découverte/IHRF, 1991, pp. 95–102; and on vengeance as a punitive practice, see also his *Il trono vuoto. La transizione della sovranità nella rivoluzione francese*, Turin: Einaudi, 1989.

was also the invention of a new place for legislators who had now to fully recognize popular sovereignty, but at the same time prevent the people from having to compromise themselves in unsustainable practices in order to found the Republic. Establishing the Terror had the aim of preventing emotion from giving rise to dissolution or massacre, symbolizing what had not been done in September 1792 and thus reintroducing a regulatory function for the Assembly. For Danton, the members of the Convention had to be 'the worthy regulators of national energy'.[13] Cambacérès questioned this new function of the Assembly in forestalling the disorders of the time by showing itself determined and courageous:

> Depositories of national sovereignty, respect yourselves sufficiently so as not to fear the immense responsibility with which you are charged. If times of revolution demand extreme measures, who should take such measures if not those men whom the nation has entrusted to care for its dearest interests?[14]

Duhem supported this new function of the representative as avenger of the people:

> When the people sent us here, they said to us, 'You have our powers: go, establish liberty, get rid of all tyranny, avenge our oppression. Sincerely avenge the people, sweep away everything that might obstruct revolutionary vengeance, expedite the performance of justice.'[15]

Contrary to the prevailing interpretations today, then, the Terror was thus aimed at establishing limits to the

---

13   *Archives parlementaires*, vol. 60, p. 17.
14   Ibid, p. 59.
15   Ibid, p. 67.

sovereign exception, putting a brake on the legitimate violence of the people and giving a public and institutionalized form to vengeance. Terror as justice was thus a desperate and despairing attempt to constrain both political crime and the legitimate popular vengeance that could result from it. As a form of exercise of power, it did not amount to a condemnation of the vengeance wreaked in September 1792, but rather of the form that this assumed as a result of the impunity in which the elites had left the counter-revolutionaries.[16]

It was not enough, however, for the Assembly to take responsibility for violence; this had to be done swiftly. When Danton demanded the creation of a revolutionary tribunal, the moderate sections, whose members did not need to work in order to live, occupied their respective assemblies in the absence of the sans-culottes. They then passed motions that the latter subsequently disavowed: 'Seeing the honest citizen occupied in his labours, the artisan busy in his workshop, they had the foolishness to believe themselves in a majority.'[17] And yet, as Danton declared: 'These enemies of liberty raise an emboldened brow; after being everywhere put to rout, they make provocations everywhere.' It was they, therefore, who risked experiencing the just vengeance of the people. 'Well and good! Uproot them yourselves for popular vengeance.'[18]

This 'uprooting' involved an arduous struggle. Time was pressing. In the report of the events of 9 September

---

16 In this respect, what René Girard says on the difference or lack of difference between vengeance and penal justice is illuminating: 'The penal system has no principle of justice essentially different from the principle of vengeance. The same principle is at work in both cases, that of violent reciprocity or retribution. Either this principle is just, and justice is already present in vengeance, or else there is no justice in either case. The English expression for vengeance is that someone "takes the law into his own hands".' *La violence et le sacré*, Paris: Grasset, 1972.
17 Danton. *Archives parlementaires*, vol. 60, p. 63 (10 March 1793).
18 Ibid.

1792 in Versailles, the mayor is portrayed in the midst of the mêlée:

> He wanted to speak, sobs stifled his voice ... he saw the massacre, he lost consciousness, he was taken into a house, he came to his senses, he wanted to leave, he was held, he said that he was dishonouring himself as a man, he wanted to die for the law. 'There's no point in trying to save them', he was told. 'There's no longer time.'[19]

This 'no longer time' is like a mirror of the phrase, 'it is time', which is characteristic of the discourse of the Terror. We find this expression in the appeal drafted by Hébert and Royer on 5 September 1793, in all the major reports of the *Comité de sureté générale* and the *Comité de salut public*. However anodyne it might appear, it was not so in practice. The revolutionary time of the Terror was one in which no one could afford to spend time in long debates, slow and laborious political considerations.[20] The translation of emotions had to be both intense and brief, imposing a regime of temporality appropriate to the lightning course of events. 'Let the sword of the law, reaching with terrible speed the heads of the conspirators, strike terror into their accomplices', Robespierre demanded on 12 August 1792.[21] On 17 Pluviôse of year II, he spoke of a 'prompt, severe and inflexible justice'.[22] Couthon made this more specific on 22 Prairial of year

---

19 *Procès-verbal des événements du 9 septembre dressé d'après le récit de monsieur le maire et de plusieurs officiers municipaux. Mémoires sur les journées de Septembre.* Cited after Conein, *Langage politique et mode d'affrontement*, p. 133.

20 A similarly long and laborious process had been needed to obtain a declaration that the *patrie* was in danger.

21 *Le Moniteur universel*, vol. 17, p. 388 (12 August 1792).

22 'Sur les principes de morale politique' (17 Pluviôse year II); Robespierre, *Pour le Bonheur et pour la Liberté*, p. 296.

II: 'The time taken to punish the enemies of the *patrie* cannot be more than that needed to recognize them; it is not so much a question of punishing as of annihilating them.'[23] The Terror presupposed quick action so as to defeat the enemies before they destroyed the Revolution; so that the people would not be disgusted by injustice, and would not have to take up again for themselves 'the sword of the law'; to spare the people from unheeding injury in their exercise of the sovereign exception, and to effectively restrain this founding sovereignty. The exercise of Terror was thus a race against time. It was undoubtedly here that the project became impossible: to give the expected justice a form that was at the same time controlled – and to do so at lightning speed.

FROM THE LAW OF SUSPECTS TO THE REORGANIZATION OF THE REVOLUTIONARY TRIBUNAL

The law of suspects, which is no less vilified than the unlimited extension of revolutionary terror, was yet, as we have seen, a means for suspending the mimetic law of spilled blood. To imprison suspects meant maintaining the race against time against the counter-revolution, without having immediate recourse to the power of 'making die'. Here we come up against the thorny question of distinguishing between the guilty and the innocent, between indulgence and severity, which re-emerged time and again in the course of the Revolution: oppression had to be resisted but, in the repression of traitors, the number of guilty liable to the death penalty had to be restricted. It was Robespierre who demanded that the Girodins be imprisoned and not executed after the insurrectionary *journées* of 31 May and 21 June 1793, when the sans-culottes, armed with their pikes, entered the Assembly to demand the

23   *Le Moniteur universel*, vol. 20, p. 695.

expulsion of the treacherous representatives. It was Robespierre once again who, on 5 Nivôse of year II (25 December 1793), explained the nature of revolutionary government and terror:

> And so, if we regarded as criminals all those who, in the revolutionary movement, exceeded the precise line drawn by prudence, we would encompass in a common proscription along with bad citizens, all the natural friends of liberty, your own friends and all the supports of the Republic . . . What can then untangle all these distinctions? What can draw the dividing line between all the contrary excesses? Love of the *patrie* and of truth. Kings and scoundrels will always seek to abolish this, they want nothing to do with either reason or truth.[24]

Such was the political wager that he spelled out again on 17 Pluviôse of year II: 'We have preferred to be guided in such stormy circumstances by love of the good and the sentiment of the needs of the *patrie*, rather than by an exact theory and precise rules of conduct.'[25] Here he showed the importance of decision in politics, a decision which then melded together with the exercise of the 'sovereign exception'.

But this exception had to remain precisely that, and the whole art of revolutionary government lay in replacing the right of nations or the right of war, which knows only the death penalty, with what could be called the right of popular vengeance, so eagerly demanded by popular spokesmen from 20 June 1792 onwards. The law of 22 Prairial year II broke precisely

---

24 Robespierre, *Pour le Bonheur et pour la Liberté*, p. 277.
25 Robespierre, 17 Pluviôse year II. *Archives parlementaires*, vol. 84, p. 330. Bronislaw Baczko seems to be commenting on this sentence when he says that 'the Terror was not the realization of a preconceived political project'; see 'The Terror Before the Terror', p. 23.

with this kind of suspense, veering completely towards the idea of an end to terror as a time of vengeance.

This law of Prairial year II produced more in the way of retrospective dread than any other measure taken under the Terror. The meaning of this sovereign 'making die' has not been handed down, which further accentuates its terrifying character. Analysis of the Terror in terms of public vengeance makes it possible to partly remove this enigma and loss of meaning. In actual fact, the reorganization of the revolutionary tribunal was prepared by Saint-Just in the month of Ventôse year II (March 1794), during the factional struggle, at the same time as he declared that 'happiness is a new idea in Europe', that 'the unfortunate are the powers of the earth', and prepared the means for compensating them by redistributing the goods of traitors (i.e. émigrés) three months before Couthon's report on the reorganization of justice and the revolutionary tribunal. When Saint-Just was working on this reorganization,[26] he envisaged sorting suspects into two categories: 'unjustly arrested patriots' and 'enemies of the Revolution detained in prison'. For the latter, the penalty was to be detention until the onset of peace, and then banishment. Saint-Just thus proposed an end to suspicion and vengeance without inflicting the death penalty. The decree he presented a month later, on 26 Germinal year II (16 April 1794), proposed the establishment of two parliamentary commissions,

> one charged with editing the laws that had been passed up until then into a succinct and complete code, suppressing those that had become confused; the other charged with drafting a body of civil institutions appropriate to preserve morality and the spirit of freedom.[27]

---

26 On this reorganization, see Françoise Brunel, *Thermidor. La chute de Robespierre*, Paris: Complexe, 1989, pp. 64, 70.

27 Saint-Just, 27 Germinal year II, *Œuvres complètes*, article 25 of

These two projects were to bring the cycle of vengeance to a close, on the one hand by presenting the sum total of laws to govern society, on the other by preparing a project of civil institutions which, by organizing festivals and public education, would bring the Revolution into popular customs. But the first commission not only prepared a code for a future time of peace, but also one for a time of war: the law of 22 Prairial year II. When Saint-Just had tackled the question of a way forward from vengeance in Ventôse, he was preparing for peace. When Couthon presented his legislative project to the Convention in Prairial, he was declaring war. Saint-Just maintained a logic of social vengeance, whilst deferring to a future peace the opportunity of brightening the political horizon and the application of a penalty that would in all cases avoid death. The law of Prairial seemed to assert that the time was no longer suited for maintaining this logic of social division and suspending the counter-offensive specific to vengeance: the only penalty retained was death, and the rule by which judgement was made was the conscience of the judge enlightened by love of justice and the *patrie*.

The revolutionary tribunal no longer obeyed rules of vengeance, but rather those of war. In this logic, the person judged was no longer assumed to belong to a common social group, he was no longer an adversary to convince or re-educate, but rather an irreconcilable enemy to be struck down rather than banished. The suspect's alterity had become radical. And the cycle of vengeance thus ended up on two opposing paths: restored peace in a society reconciled to revolutionary values and supported by civil institutions; and a declaration of war on those in the prisons who were viewed as no longer capable of adopting revolutionary values. Such statements as 'Revolution is the war of liberty

the decree on the general police, p. 822.

against its enemies' have to be taken literally. This was the logic championed by Robespierre and Saint-Just in the trial of Louis XVI, which according to them applied the right of war: Louis had to be treated as a foreigner and not as a citizen.

'Vengeance ceases to play the role of regulating violence when, transforming the adversary into an enemy, it degenerates into war and leads to his annihilation.'[28] If the period of the Terror is so difficult to grasp, this is because the logic of public vengeance and the logic of war coexist. This is particularly true for the members of the Convention who, embodying the 'whole' of the divided society, were exposed to the greatest severity. When they did not match up to the values to be founded, they fell into the camp of enemies.[29] The factional struggles in which Hébert and then Danton perished, and which are seen as fratricidal, were bound up with the necessity of not simply choosing one's camp clearly in a context of vengeance, but also of being able to embody the foundational values as representative of the people. But what matters most to my mind is that the cycle of vengeance was first opened and then closed, and that all the practices for controlling violence during the period of Terror were simply a repetition of the death of the king – from one precipice to another, as it were.[30]

One of the questions left unanswered in the interpretation of the law of Prairial is that of its political appropriateness. Why so much violence at a time when the Republic seemed to have been saved? Classically, it is easier to open a cycle of vengeance than to close it, and this cycle can become quite protracted or even never close. In that case, society will be constantly

---

28 Verdier, *La vengeance*, vol. 3, p. 152.
29 This was certainly the case with Danton.
30 In the expression of Myriam Revault d'Alonnes, *D'une mort à l'autre. Précipices de la révolution*, Paris: Esprit/Le Seuil, 1989.

subject to a bipolar and reciprocal violence between social groups that do not manage to resume living together. It is not external circumstances that enable us to grasp the logic of the moment at which this desire to close the circle appears, but rather the internal dynamic of confrontation, a conception of repression in which a right of war that is unsparing of the spillage of blood coexists with a right of vengeance that is concerned on the contrary not to 'make die'.

One way forward from vengeance amounts to declaring that popular sovereignty had been established. Yet nothing guaranteed that such sovereignty would no longer meet with irreconcilable enemies, or that the Prairial tribunal would put an end to them once and for all. Just like the Amalekites of the Old Testament who opposed the divine law and were condemned by God to be annihilated, the people's enemies could always re-emerge, and for this reason mercy was a fault.[31] As for the civil institutions that provided the other way forward from the cycle of vengeance and division, by maintaining the rediscovered social unity of French patriots and affirming the values of the Republic, they make it possible to grasp a further dimension of vengeance: assuring the foundation of a new symbolic system.

VALUES AS TOUCHSTONE

Public vengeance was a way of elaborating values and putting them to the test.[32] The great reports of year II constantly hammer home the desire to found a new

---

31   King Saul, who did not fully obey God and spared the Amalekites he had captured, himself lost his kingdom. The God of Israel no longer recognized him as the king of Israel.

32   D. Vidal, in his article 'Vengeance' in the *Dictionnaire d'anthropologie et d'ethnologie*. He goes on to note that 'it is possible to invoke texts such as the *Iliad*, the *Mahabharata* or the Old Testament, to show how the expression of values may be constantly repeated in narrative situations dominated by a context of vengeance' (p. 738).

symbolic order. But the exercise of vengeance can lead to destroying these same values by giving rise to acts that are too contrary to them. For this reason, the exercise of terror cannot be dissociated from 'morality in action'. The dynamic of the Terror does not invoke politics against morality; the politics that it practises is indissociable from the morality to be introduced.[33] As Robespierre declared to the Convention:

> Since the soul of the Republic is virtue, equality, and since your aim is to found and consolidate the Republic, it follows that the first rule of your political conduct must be to relate all your operations to the maintenance of equality and the development of virtue. With virtue and equality, therefore, you have a compass that can guide you in the midst of the storms of all passions and the whirlpool of intrigues that surround you.[34]

Decisions must therefore rest on the normative intuition of the good, or specifically that of virtue. The notion of reason is not opposed to the register of the emotions, but rather echoes it. Love of the *patrie* is the foundation of reason. The two are thus reciprocally associated and mutually reinforcing. Vengeance can only be the foundation of republican values if it is based on a moral sentiment which is posited as necessary hypothesis: 'love of the *patrie* and of truth'. What we have here, with the Terror, is a political paradigm that places sentiment rather than reason in the founding position. This is why both Robespierre and Saint-Just feared apathy more than excess: apathy risked extinguishing the burning desire to exercise sovereignty and be virtuous in the sense understood by Montesquieu:

---

33 This 'morality in action', however – the virtuous laws designed to end misfortune – most often preceded major measures of constraint.
34 Robespierre. *Archives parlementaires*, vol. 84, p. 332.

If a choice had to be made between an excess of patriotic fervour and the nothing of inactivity or the swamp
of moderation, there would be no doubt about it. A
vigorous body, tormented by an overabundance of
sap, leaves more resources than a corpse. Let us not kill
patriotism by seeking to cure it. Patriotism is ardent by
nature; who can love their *patrie* in a cold fashion?[35]

And yet public vengeance was always terrible and constituted a serious risk. The return of fear could in turn
dissolve the social and political bond. Knowledge of
the dangers of fury and the principle of mutual aid
could fail in harnessing the violence at work in revenge.
One of the essential issues in the Terror consisted precisely in forestalling and punishing any arbitrary and
bloody overflow, which in the revolutionaries' vocabulary was seen as 'anarchy'[36] or 'fury' – and in the
vocabulary of Walter Benjamin, as a mythical violence
that founds right without associating it with a principle
of justice. Over against such a foundation, the Terror
sought to give the anger of the people, as divine anger,
forms that were neither discretionary nor arbitrary.
The sacrifice of life had to be made to the benefit of a
'living-well' that neither could nor should be confused
with the simple fact of living.

For the revolutionaries, the arbitrary violence that
dissolved all social ties arose from a confusion between
private and public emotional wellsprings. With the
creation of the revolutionary tribunal and the application of the law of suspects, deputations from the
sections deplored that 'certain ill-meaning members of
the revolutionary committees are profiting from their

---

35   Ibid, p. 302.
36   On the use of this term, see Marc Deleplace, *L'anarchie de Mably
à Proudhon. Histoire d'une appropriation polémique*, Fontenay: ENS
Édition, 2000.

power to satisfy their particular revenge'.[37] Citizen Phulpin, justice of the peace for the Arcis section, had printed an *Avis à ses frères composant les comités révolutionnaires et à tous les républicains*, in which he declared:

> This is the moment at which the enemies of the public good have to be made to tremble, and all their plots stayed. This is the moment at which they must be forced to leave us free; but we must also renounce all particular vengeance in our operations.[38]

Vengeance as we come across it right through this period is public in the sense that it involves the common good of the Republic, public and not private safety. 'Popular vengeance', 'the vengeance of the laws', 'just vengeance', 'national vengeance', 'vengeance of the people' – all of these variations of the term attest to this. The nation, the people and the laws are figures of universality, of what is to be brought into being. The opposition between penal justice, which concerns both public and private interest, and revolutionary justice, was the theme of Couthon's report on the law of 22 Prairial year II:

> We have prided ourselves in being just towards individuals, without taking too much trouble to be just towards the Republic, as if the tribunals designed to punish its enemies had been established in the interest of conspirators and not for the safety of the *patrie* . . . Ordinary crimes directly injure individuals, and only

---

37 Deputation from the Luxembourg, Tuileries and Muséum sections, 1 October 1793. *Archives parlementaires*, vol. 74, pp. 384–5. Cf. Benoît Deshaye, *Législation et exécution des lois*, Master's thesis, Université de Paris VI 2001, pp. 207–13.
38 LB 41-3393. This *Avis* was dated the 24th day of the first month, i.e. 15 October 1793; see Deshaye, *Législation et exécution des lois*, p. 210.

indirectly the whole society . . . The crimes of the conspirators, on the other hand, directly threaten the
existence of society or its liberty, which comes to one
and the same thing. The lives of scoundrels are weighed
here against that of the people.[39]

We might consider the entirety of revolutionary political work as aiming to consolidate the principles
declared in 1789 and 1793, and to make these operate
as unreflecting prejudices, in other words to take them
out of the possible sphere of discussion. To bring the
Revolution into manners was in a sense to make the
violation of the declared principles painful to a revolutionary citizen, so that such a violation made him react
emotionally, as something 'insufferable' to him. The
construction of revolutionary values could thus merge
with that of the emotional and moral wellsprings of the
citizens as political actors. These wellsprings were no
longer to be individual private virtue, but rather public
virtue as socially manufactured for each person in a
society finally constituted. This social fabric was to be
constantly consolidated by the famous civil institutions
of education and festivals, aiming always to re-imprint
the founded principles. According to the letter of the
report of 18 Floréal year II (7 May 1794), 'these
national and decadal[40] festivals must create in man, as
far as moral issues are concerned, a rapid instinct that
will lead him to do good and avoid ill without the support of reasoning'. The impressive list of festivals
proposed by this decree gives an idea of the place that
moral principles were to hold, as republican principles,
in revolutionary society. The civic religion aimed to
establish virtue, i.e. love of equality, and to establish a

---

39   *Le Moniteur universel*, 22 Prairial year II, vol. 20, p. 695.
40   ['Decadal' in the sense of every ten days, the period with which the
Convention had replaced the week, as part of the new revolutionary
calendar. – D. F.]

representation of 'humanity' humanized according to the ideas of the revolutionaries of year II. This religion was not applied, so it is hard to know if it would actually have facilitated the diffusion of such a love; but it did immediately produce the hatred of its contemporary detractors, and of those historians who have commented upon it. Such a religion, indeed, touches a point that is fundamental for understanding what was at issue with the notion of a symbolic system founded on sacred and civic virtues: the articulation of recognized and shared principles, of their social and individual expression. In sum, a new symbolic system exists only if it becomes impossible or very difficult to avoid its practical imperatives, if it holds good for the whole of society and not just for one particular social group. The quest of the protagonists of the Revolution, especially in year II, was indeed to attain this point of irreversibility for a new representation of humanity, by way of a common sensibility that made laws of constraint unnecessary. But representations of humanity are never universally shared, and the sentiment of 'humanity' is never natural. To develop it, the values constructed may rest either on the primacy of political existence, or on that of life as such. I have tried to show how, for the revolutionaries, what came first was political existence. Hannah Arendt believed that a revolutionary period invents a sentiment of humanity that rests only on pity for mistreated bodies. To respond to this and propose a different vision of what she calls the social question, we must understand what the terms *people* and *equality* meant for these revolutionaries.

4

THE PEOPLE AND THE POPULAR

WHAT DID REVOLUTIONARY EQUALITY MEAN?

One of the objectives of the Terror was the unity of French patriots. Should we then consider that what was sought here was the creation of an undivided people, with the people as a whole being identified with the common people, the poor? Does it necessarily follow that the revolutionary conception of equality was the crazy equalizing idea that circulated in several playful little texts like the couplet: 'The giants must be shortened and the small lengthened, true happiness lies in everyone being the same height'? Can we consider that, beneath this fantasy, in which the hierarchy of size refers to the hierarchy of power, the revolutionaries dreamed of a people with no one left out? There is more than one reason why I see this hypothesis as untenable.

First of all, in the imaginary of the most radical revolutionaries, such as Collot d'Herbois in his *Instruction addressée aux autorités constituées au nom de la Commission temporaire de surveillance républicaine établie à Ville-Affranchie*, 'a perfect equality of happiness is unfortunately impossible among men'. The quest for equal happiness did not lie in destroying wealth, but rather in 'making inhuman monstrosities disappear from the soil of France', and in 'reducing the intervals [since] those who have grasped the spirit of the Revolution have seen a terrifying disproportion between the works of the farmer and the artisan and the modest wage they receive':

> They have seen . . . alongside a work which should always be accompanied by comfort . . . the rags of misery and the pallor of hunger; they have heard the painful complaints of need, the sharp cries of sickness . . . On the other hand, they have seen idleness and vice in the houses of wealth, all the refinement of a barbarous luxury . . . [And] finally, as the summit of infamy, they have seen the contempt of these proud men pursue the poor in their cottages, they have seen these monsters, far from grieving over the evils that their very luxury has caused, aggravate them by their disdain.[1]

Twentieth-century commentators have maintained that the desire to reduce such intervals ends up abolishing them. But this was not the logic of the revolutionary statements. Among the festivals envisaged in the decree of 18 Floréal year II, and designed to bind men together, there was one intending to celebrate and honour Misfortune. The poor were not to disappear, they were to be honoured. What was intolerable was not poverty, frugality, misfortune, but rather the indignity that the poor experienced. The question was not to abolish division amongst the people but rather to oppose labour to idleness, virtue to vice, a civilized society that assured wellbeing to all provided that they worked and a barbarous society that despised the people as an 'immense class of the poor'. As Collot put it, 'the people are above all the immense class of the poor'. This 'above all' is susceptible of much comment, but let

---

1   Commission temporaire de Ville-Affranchie, pp. 6–7.

us hold here to the letter of the text: 'above all' does not mean 'only'. The tension between the people as a whole and the common people was not abolished, but as in every political situation in which a democratic upsurge makes itself felt, the little people, the people so often left out of account, were supposed, not to become rich, but to put the rich back in their moral and political place, by asserting that wealth did not authorize them to claim more in the way of liberty and sovereignty than anyone else. If the rich were rich, this should no longer authorize them to be disdainful, oppressive and indifferent to the misfortunes of others. It was not a question of destroying the wealthy outright or even of sharing out their wealth, but rather of obliging them to become human again – in other words, solicitous of the humanity of the poor, respectful of 'the immense class of the poor'. What was hateful was not wealth as such, but its moral and political effects on those who possessed it, and its moral, political and material effects on those who experienced oppression. This was why Robespierre, on 24 April 1793, rejected the idea of an agrarian law:

> You know that this agrarian law that you have spoken so much about is simply a phantom created by rogues in order to frighten imbeciles; no revolution was needed to teach the world that the great disproportion of fortunes is the source of many evils and many crimes. But we are no less convinced that equality of goods is a chimera. The point is more to render poverty honourable than to proscribe opulence.[2]

On 17 June 1793, Robespierre opposed the idea that the people should be relieved of contributing to public expenditures, with these being borne solely by the rich:

---

2 Maximilien Robespierre, *Œuvres complètes*, vol. 9, Paris: E. Leroux, 1910, p. 459.

I am enlightened by the good sense of the people, who
feel that the kind of favour that would be done to them
in this way is in fact no more than an injury. It would
establish a class of proletarians, a class of helots, and
equality as well as liberty would perish for all time.[3]

Liberty in this speech is not opposed to equality; it is its
guarantee. Liberty is the property of the citizen who
takes part in sovereignty, and the common people are
'simply free *like* the rest'.[4] This is not an equality of
the market, in which profits and debts are redistrib-
uted, but rather a political equality that becomes at the
same time a quality of the people as a whole and the
sole quality of the free common people. The revolutionary configuration was that described by Jacques
Rancière when he proposed a definition of democracy
in which 'the demos attributes to itself as its proper lot
the equality that belongs to all citizens'.[5]

That is the fundamental wrong . . . the people appropriate the common quality as their own . . . The
qualification that they bring is a contentious property
since it does not belong exclusively to the people, but
this contentious property is strictly speaking only the
setting-up of a contentious commonality. The mass of
men without qualities identify with the community in
the name of the wrong that is constantly being done to
them by those whose position or qualities have the
natural effect of propelling them into the nonexistence
of those who have 'no part in anything'.

Rancière maintains that a democratic politics exists
when those with 'no part' have a part, i.e. 'the inter-
ruption of the simple effects of domination by the

---

3 Robespierre, *Archives parlementaires*, vol. 9, pp. 575–6.
4 Rancière, *Disagreement*, p. 8.
5 Ibid.

rich . . . causes the poor to exist as an entity'.[6] And further: 'The people are not one class among others. They are the class of the wrong that harms the community and establishes it as a "community" of the just and the unjust.'[7]

Revolutionary equality does not conceal within it egalitarianism. Equality is rather the classical expression of a democratic upsurge, the principle that authorizes the *demos* to take power over the aristocrats and the rich. This is the sense in which we should understand Saint-Just's famous sentence: 'The poor are the powers of the earth, they have the right to speak as masters to governments that neglect them.' The poor referred to here were not suffering bodies but beings of speech, they even disposed of what we can call a sovereign speech, they were those who disposed of the political *logos* even if they were not the executive power, the government that may always be negligent. This can be called rhetoric or poetry, but we need to take this proposition seriously in order to analyze the way in which the revolutionary dynamic made this power effective – a power transformed from unhappy and complaining bodies into a people disposing of powerful political *logos*.

The emergence of this political *logos* did not wait for 1793; it was present already in the *cahiers de doléances* of 1789. At Le Mesnil Saint-Germain, we find the following statement: 'The life of the poor must be more sacred than a part of the property of the rich.' But it was in the debate of the Constituent Assembly over the right of petition that a cleavage emerged between a conception in which the people were sovereign and another conception in which they were simply the object of policy. The one side sought to separate the suffering body of the poor with their complaints from the

6 Ibid., p. 11.
7 Ibid., p. 9.

political institution of the people. This was the position of Le Chapelier, who wanted to reserve the right of petition to active citizens, and make a radical distinction between this and the notion of complaint. The other side set out to politicize complaint by considering it as always having the value of a political address, and thus right from the start a political speech that must belong to all citizens. This was the position of Robespierre and of Abbé Grégoire. In the words of the latter:

> I know in Paris citizens who are not active, who live in a sixth-floor attic and are for all that able to give enlightenment and useful opinion (*applause from the benches*). Would you reject these citizens? ... They will address themselves to you in order to claim their rights when they have been slighted, as the Declaration of Rights is after all common to all men. Will you refuse to hear their demands? Will you then regard their sighs as acts of rebellion, their complaints as an attack against the laws? And whom would we prohibit non-active citizens from addressing? Administrators, municipal officials, those who should be the defenders of the people, the guardians and fathers of the poor. Is not complaint a natural right? And should a citizen not have, precisely because he is poor, the right of soliciting protection from the public authority? ... If you deprive the poor citizen of the right to present petitions, you detach him from public affairs, you even make him their enemy. Unable to complain in legal ways, he will resort to tumultuous movements and replace reason by despair ... The freedom to think and to express his thinking in any way whatsoever is the lever of political liberty.[8]

It is in the details of these debates that we can observe the manner in which the entrance of the poor onto the political stage was conceived. For the protagonists of

---

8   *Le Moniteur universel*, vol. 8, p. 354.

the Constituent Assembly, there was not a politics of pity but two different modes of refusal. The first refusal lay simply in completely ignoring the poor, who were to be neither subjects nor objects of politics, but relegated as passive citizens unable to expect equality or to exercise their free judgement or speech. The second was to maintain that it was unacceptable to refuse the poor the right of petition, i.e. refuse their becoming political subjects in the full sense, subjects of liberty. If politics began at the point when the trembling of the living body could be converted into political *logos*, then to maintain a natural right of petition for all human beings amounted to refusing that being a citizen meant no more than enjoying the 'fine day of life'. From grievance to petition, the revolutionary movement politicized the living.

Analysis of the Declaration of the Rights of Man and of the Citizen offers a further argument against the hypothesis of a levelling egalitarianism. This 'recognizes no other distinctions than that of talent and virtue'.[9] This is why the project of an indivisible people was not the project of a people as *one*, in the sense that psychoanalysts speak of a fusion between people. Not only do gaps exist between human beings, but these are magnified in the quest for endless ascent onto the rock of the rights of man – which, despite being declared, are never definitively won. Being virtuous meant making a constant effort in this endless ascent: Chaumette spoke of the 'Mount Sinai of the French people'.[10] And if the people were to 'identify themselves with their constitution', it was in this political and moral effort, the effort of an ever precarious liberty that had to be hotly defended, and that shifted with the tides of history not only the intervals of

---

9   Declaration of the Rights of Man and of the Citizen, article VI.
10   From a speech of 5 September 1793, as printed in *Le Journal de la Montagne*, 6–7 September 1793.

happiness between men, but also the border between the left and right sides of political sensibility. We are far here from a conception in which the right of the wretched to existence transforms the people into a powerless and ultimately oppressed mass. In the revolutionary utterance, 'the people' exists only by reference to values that found it as subject of liberty and dignity. It is ultimately the name of people that concretizes the idea of a human race that regains its rights and its human nature, in a democratic action with universal value.

When Arendt talks of the language of passion in connection with revolutionary cruelty, she associates this with pity for the less fortunate and declares that such cruelty is as boundless as misfortune. Yet if there is a language of passion, this is not passion for a social question independent of politics, but rather passion for right, for the Declaration of Rights that was not only to put an end to the misfortunes of the poor, but also to the misfortunes of peoples – which, we recall, have as their cause 'the ignorance, neglect or contempt of the natural rights of man', which are 'liberty, security, property and resistance to oppression'.[11] Nor should we forget that, in the preamble to the same Declaration of 1789, it is asserted that the objective is to ensure that 'the grievances of the citizens, based hereafter upon simple and incontestable principles, shall tend to the maintenance of the constitution and redound to the happiness of all'.

This question of natural rights being declared for the protection of the people is a fundamental one, since those who betray these rights provoke the sovereign exception as divine violence, along with the cruelty that necessarily accompanies it – we understand today the limitations of the guillotine's lack of cruelty, or indeed those of the lethal injection of American executions.

---

11   Preamble to the Declaration of the Rights of Man and of the Citizen.

In this culture of inalienable and sacred natural right, the border between identity and alterity separates men in the wild state, who do not have access to right, from civilized men familiar with this. On this border there are two categories of man. The first is composed of those who learn or discover the rules of natural right, become citizens and expand the ranks of the sovereign. The second is composed of men who know right but do not apply it. These are traitors to the nation, and more generally traitors to humanity.

To betray humanity, in revolutionary logic, means knowing right but not respecting it, preferring to it the use of force. Betraying humanity means not defending right against those who attack it, or preventing ignorant men from discovering it.

Robespierre, in the constitutional debates of spring 1793, expressed a fundamental analogy between relations among states and relations among citizens:

> The men of all countries are brothers, and must help one another as citizens of a single state. Whoever oppresses one nation declares himself the enemy of all. Those who wage war on a people, in order to halt the progress of liberty and destroy the rights of man, must be pursued everywhere not as ordinary enemies, but as assassins and rebel brigands.[12]

(We find again here the figure of the brigand, which at this time denoted anyone who placed himself outside the social bond, outside common humanity, despite knowing its rules. The first individual in the French Revolution to embody this position was King Louis XVI, the figure of traitor par excellence.)

The first element in the tradition of natural right that we need to dwell on here is the one that makes it possible to understand on what condition the death of

---

12   Robespierre, *Pour le Bonheur et pour la Liberté*, p. 233.

the enemy was necessary. For Locke, it was those who were harmful to common humanity who had to be destroyed:

> And that all men may be restrained from invading others' rights, and from doing hurt to one another, and the law of nature be observed, which willeth the peace and *preservation of all mankind*, the *execution* of the law of nature is, in that state, put into every man's hands, whereby every one has a right to punish the transgressors of that law to such a degree, as may hinder its violation . . .
>
> In transgressing the law of nature, the offender declares himself to live by another rule than that of reason and common equity, which is that measure God has set to the actions of men, for their mutual security; and so he becomes dangerous to mankind, the tye, which is to secure them from injury and violence, being slighted and broken by him. Which being a trespass against the whole species, and the peace and safety of it, provided for by the law of nature, every man upon this score, by the right he hath to preserve mankind in general, may restrain, or where it is necessary, destroy things noxious to them, and so may bring such evil on any one, who hath transgressed that law, as may make him repent the doing of it, and thereby deter him, and by his example others, from doing the like mischief.[13]

Locke introduces here the reciprocity of natural right, reason as law of nature, and the concept of the human race as political entity. This last point was not his invention, as the Stoics were the first to trace the limit beyond which a man removes himself from the universal community of men, becoming *inhumanum* relative to the *genus humanum*. Anyone who puts their own

13   John Locke, *Second Treatise on Government*, London: A. Millar et al., 1764 Book 1, chap. 2, paras 7 and 8.

interest above that of others acts inhumanely, with a lack of respect for natural law. We find in Cicero the necessary exclusion of the inhuman, when the human race is a political concept:

> As certain members [of the body] are amputated, if they show signs ... of being bloodless and virtually lifeless and thus jeopardize the health of the other parts of the body, so those fierce and savage monsters in human form [such as the tyrant Phalaris] should be cut off from what may be called the common body of humanity.[14]

A person with whom any community is impossible must be killed.

In the state of the modern period, positive right is not applied to those who do not respect right, i.e. who do not respect their own laws. Nor again is it applied to those who are not given to right and remain brigands, outside of right government. It is then natural right that is applied, and this right knows only the penalty of death.

When a people is constituted – that is, ordered by the principle of sovereignty – it is collectively responsible for maintaining this sovereign order, maintaining the laws. Within this space of sovereignty, responsibility is collective. Someone who does not rise up against tyrant and crime, but allows crimes to happen, himself becomes a tyrant and a traitor. 'The cruelty of pity' is therefore not just a figure of rhetoric; it means that allowing political crime means becoming criminal oneself. The logic of natural right thus associates a theoretical humanism (it is in the name of humanity that one must act) with a situational anti-humanism (the life of a man or a people is worth nothing if they betray their humanity). The sentiment of revolutionary humanity does not lead to

---

14 *De Officiis* III,6.32; see Cicero, *De Officiis*, trans. W. Miller, London: William Heinemann, 1968, pp. 298–9.

protecting suffering bodies above everything else, regardless of who and where they might be. The object is to protect above all humanity as a group constituted politically by its respect for declared natural right, from the most local to the most cosmopolitan level. We might say that this sentiment of humanity is entirely on the side of political life, sometimes accepting the need to despise the 'fine day of life' that may conceal within it the oppression of the whole human race.

Revolutionary pity does not wish to make poverty disappear, to exclude it from the community, but on the contrary to give it a place that makes insensitivity towards it impossible. To maintain the human identity of all does not therefore mean fantasizing a people identified with the poor, which would suppose *a contrario* destroying the rich and their wealth. What is imperative here is to maintain that political power does not lie on the side of wealth, but rather on the side of a generalized emancipation – in other words, an emancipation of the poor. Poverty is an aspect of the trajectory of life and fate, but it should not lead to indignity. Thus the passion of the revolutionaries was not passion for the poor, but rather passion for declared, inviolable and sacred rights, the passion for justice and equality. These were the values, rather than a homogenizing egalitarianism, that founded human identity as an identity in which life was worth nothing if there was no respect for the rights that transformed it into a universal political existence.

THERMIDOR

With Thermidor, citizens had to renounce the expression of their point of view; they no longer had access to the political *logos*. In terms of the deputy Rouzet, 'the citizen must not be tempted to substitute reasoning for the submission that he owes to the law'.[15] Rejection of

---

15 *Le Moniteur universel*, vol. 25, p. 149.

the revolutionary democratic model in which, in the face of governments that were always assumed to be fallible, each citizen was responsible for maintaining the rights of man and the citizen, was the Thermidorian characteristic. It was accompanied by rejection of universal suffrage, and of those reforms of civil law that led to more egalitarian practices between men and women, as well as among heirs with a view to reducing the disparities of wealth that resulted from birth.[16] As for the rejection of revolutionary violence – in particular the September massacres, the death of the king, the Terror – this was the basis for political struggles between Girondins and Montagnards, then between indulgence and inflexible severity. Thermidor seemed to mean the triumph of the Girondins, but gradually, under cover of a struggle against anarchy, it was the entire Revolution that the monarchists of the Directory period sought to disqualify. Their notion of anarchy was initially extremely plastic and polysemic. In year II, the word 'anarchy' had disappeared from the political vocabulary. It made its return in Germinal year III (March–April 1795) when, against the sections of the east of Paris who demanded 'bread and the constitution of 1793', anarchy was identified with the 'system of Robespierre' or the 'regime of 1793', and the anarchist with the 'drinker of blood'. 'Anarchy' thus became the expression of a social fear, the fear of the class of property owners who were marked by the trauma of the Terror; its spectres had the names of Equality and Agrarian Law. The anarchist was then placed outside the social law and outside the law of nature: he was a monster. And in year VII, the royalists finally managed to wrap up the whole of the Revolution and the republicans under the name of an anarchy that went back to 14 July 1789. Nevertheless, for those who

---

16   On the Thermidorian backlash, see Suzanne Desan, 'Reconstituting the social after the Terror: family, property and the law in popular politics', *Past and Present* 164 (1999), pp. 81–121.

remained republicans, the infamy that weighed on the Terror of 1793 still spared the earlier period of the Revolution. Jourdan could still maintain in the Assembly that '14 July and 10 August were days of anarchy in which the people regained their rights, and in this way shared in the events for which the Republicans claim the honour'. We find here once again the division between the wheat and the chaff that was to mark the bicentenary of the French Revolution.

The division of sensibility, if there can be said to have been such a division after Thermidor, was based on the aestheticizing of the dead body and the fear that ensued from this, without the death evoked being allowed to take on a political meaning. To show, and even present, the bodies of the guillotined or the massacred – like the duchesse de Lamballe – produced retrospective dread and the relief of having escaped the barbarism of the 'drinkers of blood'. The sans-culotte who, in the Thermidorian caricature, asks his victim to drink a glass of blood 'bottoms up'[17] is a figure devoid of political character, a mere barbarian whose rage can find no satisfactory explanation. What is constructed here is a morbid aestheticizing of the period of Terror, but also of all the actors who made the Revolution from 1789 to 1794. The abolition of the political meaning of death meted out makes this death no longer a historic and political fact, but simply an anthropological one in the sense of the eighteenth century, when this discipline separated off from history and was deemed to be a science of human nature. From this point on, man could no longer hope for happiness here on earth, and could not forget that he was not only a being-for-death but

---

17   On this representation of the sans-culotte, see Michel Naudin, 'La réaction culturelle en l'an III: la repésentation du jacobin et du sans-culotte dans l'imaginaire de leurs adversaires', in M. Vovelle (ed.), *Le tournant de l'an III. Reaction et terreur blanche dans la France révolutionnaire*, Paris: Éditions du CTHS, 1997, pp. 279–93.

also a being-for-being-put-to-death by his fellows. This negation of the meaning of the revolutionary period made way for a providentialism 'which made meaningless any human desire for earthly happiness'.[18] The counter-revolution thus made its bed out of mourning and suffering, which were all the more absolute – and one might even say pleasurable – in that they remained deprived of meaning, while happiness escaped human desires by its very nature. The death of the king had to be made into an irremediable loss, and to be mourned along with the families of the victims of the guillotine. Where the death of the political Other had constituted a sign of the exercise of legitimate right, there were now only victims to be wept over. Thermidor inaugurated for our age the reign of emotional victimhood. If there was competition, it was no longer to produce a hierarchy of heroes or martyrs, but rather a hierarchy of victims. Only those who had suffered by losing a loved one to the guillotine could drown their sorrows at certain balls that were reserved for them, where they aestheticized their status by wearing the famous thread of red silk against their bare necks.

Thermidor thus effected an initial shift towards a notion of the Revolution as incomprehensible and disastrous, by at once denying the meaning of the sovereign 'making die' and making death during the revolutionary period into a death devoid of meaning.

It became hard then to voice one's support for the constitution of 1793 and the revolutionary people without the risk of losing one's life. This was true not just for the insurgents of Prairial year III (May 1795), who demanded bread and the 1793 constitution and were bloodily repressed, but also for those members of the Convention who wanted to hear and translate this demand that had become intolerable. Whereas in 1792

popular spokesmen emerged, steadily shifted the reception of popular emotions and managed to offer them a
place, in Prairial the Montagnard deputies who played
this role were immediately disavowed and their actions
criminalized. In prison, they chose to kill themselves in
the name of the flouted principles. The republican tradition remembers them as the 'martyrs of Prairial'. For a
deputy to offer a place to popular emotions had become
a criminal act before its political significance was even
discussed. The deputies to the Convention would no
longer be translators of popular emotions, but had to
reject any exchange with the people. Thus, on the *journée*
of 1 Prairial, Boissy d'Anglas refused a dialogue with the
insurgents. The accounts of this *journée* put forward the
rule: popular anger had become intolerable, the people
were denied any normative value in terms of justice.

Here we touch on a fundamental point in the
Thermidorian enterprise. The operation of repressing
emotions was accompanied by an important political
translation: the Declaration of Rights and the constitution were changed. The legislative demands that the
people could bear within their sovereign emotive movement were always linked to the notion of resistance to
oppression. In June 1792, reference to article 2 of the
Declaration was perfectly explicit:

> In the name of the nation, which has its eyes fixed on
> this city, we come to assure you that the people are
> standing up, as circumstances require, and ready to use
> major means to avenge the outraged national majesty.
> These rigorous means are justified by article 2 of the
> Rights of Man: *resistance to oppression*.[19]

This image of 'the people standing up', as opposed to
an enslaved people on its knees, reappears in the
journées of Prairial in the following variant: 'We have

---

19   *Archives parlementaires*, vol. 45, p. 146.

stood up in order to support the Republic and liberty.' This expression gave the signal for popular uprising, for the attempt to resist oppression. And this element of article 2 of the 1789 Declaration, resistance to oppression as an inalienable and sacred right, was abolished by the writers of the constitution of year III, along with article 35 that spoke of the duty of insurrection.

On 5 Messidor of year III, Boissy d'Anglas spoke to the Constituent Assembly as follows:

> You will understand that it is immoral, impolitic and excessively dangerous to establish in a constitution such a damaging principle of disorganization as that which provokes insurrection against the actions of any government . . . We have thus suppressed article 35 which was the work of Robespierre, and which, in more than one circumstance, became the rallying cry of brigands armed against you.[20]

Daunou, in a debate on article 2 on 16 Messidor (4 July 1795), declared that

> the commission [of eleven] had suppressed from article 2 of the Declaration of Rights only the statement of the right of resistance to oppression, which it had seen as presenting too great a danger and as opening the door to too much abuse.[21]

What had been the foundation of the juridical legitimacy of the revolutionary movement had thus become intolerable.

---

20 *Le Moniteur universel*, vol. 25, p. 81; reprinted Paris: Plon, 1947. On the position of Boissy d'Anglas, see Yannick Bosc, 'Boissy d'Anglas et le rejet de la Déclaration de 1793', in Roger Bourderon (ed.), *L'an I et l'apprentissage de la démocratie*, Saint-Denis: Éditions PSD, 1995.
21 *Le Moniteur universel*, vol. 25, p. 151.

CONCLUSION:
THE TERROR AND TERRORISM

The revolutionary Terror, which is attacked for its revolutionary tribunal, its law of suspects and its guillotine, was a process welded to a regime of popular sovereignty in which the object was to conquer tyranny or die for liberty. This Terror was willed by those who, having won sovereign power by dint of insurrection, refused to let this be destroyed by counter-revolutionary enemies. The Terror took place in an uncertain struggle waged by people who tried everything to deflect the fear felt towards the counter-revolutionary enemy into a terror imposed on it. This enemy, for its part, tried everything to bring the Revolution to an end. The greatest danger was then that of a weakening of the revolutionary desire – a discouragement, a corruption of the founding desire. It was this danger that haunted those actors most committed to the revolutionary process.

This is why the Terror was a deliberate self-constraint: it was not just a policy of arbitrary violence or extreme fear to intimidate its enemies. It was the historic moment when the sovereign violence of 'making die' was that of a people driven to make use of it to maintain the extraordinary claim to have conquered sovereignty.

'The abyss of the Terror' is never completely closed, as this unlikely encounter between the political and the sacred remains fascinating and disturbing. Kant commented on the 'sympathy of admiration' aroused by the French Revolution in terms of 'enthusiasm' and the 'moral disposition of the human race' – even if 'a sensible man would never resolve to attempt the experiment at such cost'. This moral disposition is what the revolutionaries called the sentiment of humanity. The experiment of the revolution, according to Kant, was thus not a loss of the sentiment of humanity, but on the contrary precisely a sign of this.

'Citizens, what illusion managed to persuade you that you were inhuman?' Saint-Just exclaimed on 8 Ventôse year II (26 February 1794):

> Your revolutionary tribunal has dispatched 300 scoundrels in the last year; did not the Spanish inquisition do more? And for what cause, in the name of God! And did the English courts execute no one this year? . . . And no one mentions the German prisons in which the people are buried.[1]

What then was the price of the Terror? The classic response is that the two months between 22 Prairial and 9 Thermidor year II saw 1,376 people perish on the scaffold.[2] And brutal as the summary measures of the revolutionary tribunal then were, they were not the only price of the Terror or of the Revolution. This price also involved infringing the political border of the sacred. Fear, disgust, terror and enthusiasm were the emotions that signalled the experience of this border,

---

1 Saint-Just, *Œuvres complètes*, p. 700.
2 We should, however, bear in mind the proportions of cruelty involved: the repression of the Paris Commune left 20,000 dead, as pointed out by Jean-Pierre Faye in the article 'Terreur' in his *Dictionnaire politique portatif en cinq mots*, Paris: Gallimard, 1982.

the place where the Revolution and its actors might tumble into the void, where the violence inflicted on the body of the enemy was linked with a foundational vengeance and with popular sovereignty.

The members of the Convention wanted to protect the people from the injury of this sacred deed by focusing it in the Convention itself, its committees and the revolutionary tribunal. But no one was truly protected from a sacred transaction in which the foundation of values required the death of men, in which body and soul had to be committed, and anyone could perish from fear or be overcome by disgust. This in my view is the forgotten price of the Revolution, the buried price of the Terror – a price that is indissociably moral and political at once,[3] and that lies in discomfort, risk and a gamble.

'Terrorism' and 'terrorists' are words that originated with Thermidor. Those who sought to found a new and egalitarian political and symbolic space were defeated by history. The terrorists meant Robespierre and Saint-Just, but also all who fought for 'liberty or death' – the Jacobins whose club was closed, the citizens reduced to political passivity by the establishment of a property-based suffrage and the abolition of the right of resistance to an oppression which refused them any active citizenship. The terrorists were all those who were referred to as 'men of blood', those whose cruelty – cold or intoxicated, depending on whether they gave or fulfilled commands – came to be stigmatized as one that in every case saw politics only as a pretext to assuage a passion for blood. The Terror would be the name given by history to this period of

---

3   Maurice Merleau-Ponty, seeking to conceive the paradoxical ties between humanism and terror, noted that it is sometimes 'allowable to sacrifice those who according to the logic of their situation are a threat and to promote those who offer a promise of humanity'. *Humanism and Terror*, Boston: Beacon Press, 1969, p. 110.

'terrorism'. The view of year II of the Republic as a period of terror and dread is essentially Thermidorian.

By inventing the neologism 'terrorist', the Thermidorians not only anthropologized a violence that was also seen as popular, but they actively obscured what had given this terror a situational legitimacy: a juridico-political process of collective responsibility. In fact, the duty of insurrection made each person a watchman who had either to rise up at the risk of his life, or take responsibility for the decisions of the national Convention.[4]

Active forgetting is what is effected after the time of foundation, when the notion of the irreconcilable enemy becomes obsolete and intolerable. From this point on, the 'terrorists' were the Other of the republicans. The most fervent of these, such as Victor Hugo – little suspected of counter-revolutionary ideology – constantly asserted that, even faced with a crime such as that of 2 December 1851, they would never call for revolutionary terror. The acts of those defeated by history became infamous for those of their heirs who might be of a mind to repeat them. Even if they were understood – and Hugo's 1793 bears witness to this – no situation could lead to their repetition. Even those responsible for defending revolutionary memory knew that the foundational time was not replayable, and that such acts of terror now belonged to a different age.

'What difference does it make whether one dies from plague or revolution? Moral nature (or history) does not have to be any more moral than physical nature.' This is the argument attributed to Saint-Just by Georg Büchner in *Dantons Tod* (Danton's Death; 1834–5), in this way championing the Thermidorian view. This has

---

4 On the question of the right of resistance to oppression, see Jean-Claude Zancarini (ed.), *Le droit de résistance, XIIe-XXe siècle*, Paris: ENS Éditions, 1999; and specifically my article there on the Thermidorian repression of the right of resistance.

recently been reprised in *Le Monde*'s op-ed section, where a certain philosopher claimed to make Saint-Just speak about the events of 11 September 2001.[5] We are thus faced with a double condensation: the language of the nineteenth century founds the representation of those events of the eighteenth century that composed the 'French Revolution', and more precisely, the 'revolutionary Terror'. This representation, not made specific, but cited as a source by the author of this text, is supposed to be able to inform us about what happened on '9/11'. To make a contemporary moralizing use of this literary text under cover of a source means introducing political confusion over what meaning to give to acts of cruelty in history, and deploring a non-meaning that one has oneself put forward. For nowadays, it does not matter which body is cruelly affected and for what reason; the only worthwhile thing is the 'beautiful day of life', whatever this might be. To destroy it always means producing a victim and becoming guilty. Walter Benjamin protested against this kind of morality. In his text on violence and law, in fact, Benjamin criticized a 'theorem' that has become a virtual rule in the West, namely

> the sanctity of life, which they either apply to all animal and even vegetable life, or limit to human life. Their argument, exemplified in an extreme case by the revolutionary killing of the oppressor, runs as follows: 'If I do not kill, I shall never establish the world dominion of justice . . . that is the argument of the intelligent terrorist . . . We, however, profess that higher even than the happiness and justice of existence stands existence itself.'[6]

---

5   I am in debt to Françoise Brunel for the clarification of his pseudo-quotation by Monique Canto-Sperber, who clearly lacked a gift for Saint-Just's language.

6   Kurt Hiller, Munich 1919; cited by Benjamin in 'Critique of Violence', pp. 250–1.

For Benjamin, however,

> the proposition that existence stands higher than a just
> existence is false and ignominious, if existence is to
> mean nothing other than mere life . . . Man cannot, at
> any price, be said to coincide with the mere life in him,
> any more than it can be said to coincide with any other
> of his conditions and qualities, including even the
> uniqueness of his bodily person.[7]

'Terrorist' is thus used as a normative disqualification
which proclaims both the intolerable character of the
danger that circulates and traverses exposed bodies,
and the de-legitimation by the Thermidorian victors of
a sovereign violence, practised yesterday by the legiti-
mately elected representatives of the people who are
now turned into defeated terrorists, retrospectively
criminalized and excluded from the legal and legiti-
mately political field. The terrorist is someone
potentially defeated and always outside the law.

The term has been often recycled. It was a label used
for *résistants* who proclaimed, at the cost of their lives,
that they were not yet defeated under the regimes of
occupation and collaboration during the Second World
War. In Algeria, again, those who proclaimed the
necessity of ending the second-class citizenship that
France then offered its colonial subjects were 'terrorists'. Likewise all who sought to found the possibility
of a politics that stood against the domination experienced by the conquered. As well as those who were
known, from 1969 on, as 'hijackers'.

Revolutionary terror is not terrorism. To make a
moral equivalence between the Revolution's year II
and September 2001 is historical and philosophical
nonsense. Is this the effect of what we have called the
persistence in vision of the image of revolutionary

---

7   Benjamin, 'Critique of Violence', p. 251.

terror? The point is to note the effects of this disturbance of vision on the moral appreciation of various
political cruelties that have been practised, and still are
practised, around victors and the defeated, the perpetrators and victims of the events of 9/11. If care is not
taken, this deadly ballet could become unending.

The events of 9/11 have not yet found a name. They
are spoken of as a fascinating shock, with all that such
fascination means in terms of ambivalence: the irresist-
ible attraction of seeing and the privation of defensive
reaction.

Under Thermidor, such fascination with the representation of cruelty was not deployed immediately, in
real time, but after the event. What has since been constantly represented as object for this fascination are the
massacres. The September massacres, the Nantes *noya-
des*, the forests of guillotines . . . the tale of cruelty
offered as the only image of the Revolution, the only
fascinating explanation of this history with its trail of
victims and executioners.

In September 2001, the image preceded the story,
fascination with cruelty preceded analysis and political
judgement. But if such deprecation and disgust attest
to some people's inability to understand, these sentiments cannot completely obscure a different reception
of these events. We saw the 'V' of victory in Nigeria
and Palestine, while adolescents in Seine Saint-Denis –
department 93! – chose to write in the name of Bin
Laden on their voting slips for the election of school
councillors. Commentaries from several countries of
the global South immediately gave these events a
dimension of implicit revenge against the imperial
domination of a hegemonic political model. The dis-
symmetry of weapons no longer seems an obstacle in
causing the eternal victor to bend. It is less a question
of approving this cruel decision than of declaring that
the United States also shares responsibility for it.

Rather than proposing an explanation for the

decision in favour of terrorism, we should grasp in relief how this enabled those who never have access to public speech to take hold of this, to make known through it what is happening today on the side of those left out of account. If the French Revolution can help in analyzing such events, this is perhaps in the connection between the public speech of the voiceless, the 'understanding nothing' of this speech by those who make politics, and certain events of cruelty.

The absence of public spaces in which popular speech could beat a path for itself, be heard and echoed in the form of pacifying laws, is partly linked with the upsurge of violence. When it is no longer possible to have insurrection recognized as such, violence can no longer be restrained and bloodshed is no longer unanimously reproved.

A DIFFERENT POLITICAL SACRALITY

After 11 September 2001, New York experienced a 'state of dread'. Disturbance and discouragement came in the wake of the large number of dead and this massdeath's effect of de-subjectification. As the target of these attacks, the 'sacred body' of the United States had been assassinated. The question was how to rediscover courage after the misfortune. Such was the rhetoric of the discourse that followed, starting with George W. Bush's speech to the joint houses of Congress and the nation on 20 September 2001.

The American sacred body is of course the centre of commerce, the fetish of capitalism, the government in Washington, the presidential and military power, but above all – one might say, before all else – the bodies of the dead. In the *New York Times*, it was the 'beautiful day in the life' of the dead that had become the sacred body of the American nation. Each of these 'beautiful days' was reconstituted in a little story which, narrating marriage proposals, diseases overcome, beloved children, memories of childhood, spoke this sacrality. It was one of an ordinary humanity that now founded an indescribable or undiscoverable citizenship. Whereas in the eighteenth century, it was by becoming a citizen that the humanity of humanity was attained, everything here seems to say that it is as a human being without civic history that the sacrality of the political body was is attained. These stories constitute so many little cenotaphs for the dead, who, in their multiplicity, speak the sacred identity of the American nation. It was in the face of this profaned sacrality that Americans had to rediscover energy against discouragement.

Bush set out above all else to describe the operations that made this subjective reprise possible. He opened his speech on 20 September with what would replace the funerals that were impossible: 'We have seen the state of our union in the endurance of rescuers working past exhaustion.' The rescue operations made possible a sublimation in the event. Bush could then reconnect with the aesthetic of emotional heroizing. He closed his speech with an anecdote worthy of a funeral oration for simple heroes:

> And I will carry this. It is the police shield of a man named George Howard who died at the World Trade Center trying to save others. It was given to me by his mom, Arlene, as a proud memorial to her son. It is my reminder of lives that ended and a task that does not end.

In this unending task, the grief of a mother could be redeemed by her heroic pride, and it became imaginable again for Americans to 'die for the country'. The break this made with the First Gulf War and the intervention in Kosovo was evidence of this:

> Now, this war will not be like the war against Iraq a decade ago, with a decisive liberation of territory and a swift conclusion. It will not look like the air war

above Kosovo two years ago, where no ground troops were used and not a single American was lost in combat.

The assault on the sacred body of the beautiful day of life brings a resurgence of the sacred body of the heroic citizen, whether for a civilian or a military task.

A different sacrality – that of religion – is associated with this political sacrality in the moment of dread. The 'lighting of candles', 'the saying of prayers in English, Hebrew and Arabic' find a place in Bush's speech, which offers a manner of employing the subjective reprise as a return of ardour around these modalities of the sacred. In order to evoke the gaping profanation of the sacrality of the beautiful day of life, Bush declared: 'I ask you to live your lives and hug your children . . . I ask you to continue to support the victims of this tragedy with your contributions.' The sacrality of the country is evoked more discreetly, as it is not so easy today to maintain that there are values justifying a human death. The statement here remains elliptical: 'I ask you to uphold the values of America.' Finally, religion remains a point of support that ties together all the infringed sacralities: 'Please continue praying for the victims of terror and their families, for those in uniform and for our great country. Prayer has comforted us in sorrow and will help strengthen us for the journey ahead.'

What is sought here is thus a transmutation of the discouragement linked with fear into the will to act. What this speech aims to display is indeed that decisive shift of 'being in fear'.

> Tonight, we are a country awakened to danger and called to defend freedom. Our grief has turned to anger and anger to resolution. Whether we bring our enemies to justice or bring justice to our enemies, justice will be done.

Anger and justice were also the key words of the 'terror-response' of the French revolutionaries, but the forms and sites of profaned sacrality have fundamentally changed. Where formerly it was an attack on the body that represented the political project, represented the Declaration of the Rights of Man and of the Citizen, which called for heroism in the face of profanation, now it is an attack on the body that represents a humanism outside of politics which presupposes this resort to heroism. These bodies divested of their responsibility for common political existence are the effective representation of the American political project – a project that assumes that the veritable mode of liberty consists in no longer acknowledging any such responsibility. This absence of knowledge leads to a disinterest in the lives of others, in their equal or unequal value. The desire to promote equality in free action on a cosmopolitan scale now appears inconceivable.

The Americans responded to this 'being in fear' just as the French revolutionaries had done. If there is an analogy to be drawn between 1793 and 2001, this should be sought in a common resistance to discouragement. But the reprise of courage does not have the same sense at these different dates. The Americans, despite what they say, do not live in a time of foundation, and we have not finished observing the forms of dread that the American response has provoked – the dread of a violence that is not foundational but policing, and recently also preventive.

A reading of Benjamin offers bearings as we seek to orient a judgement of cruelties both past and present: 'For a cause, however effective, becomes violent, in the precise sense of the word, only when it enters into moral relations. The sphere of these relations is defined by the concepts of law and justice.'[8] Right and justice,

---

8 Ibid., p. 236.

however, are values that disappear in the response to contemporary terrorism, a response that is no longer founded on justice but invents the legal rules necessary for repression; as is happening at Guantánamo.

> The ignominy of such an authority [as the police] . . . lies in the fact that in this authority the separation of lawmaking and law-preserving violence is suspended. If the first is required to prove its worth in victory, the second is subject to the restriction that it may not set itself new ends. Police violence is emancipated from both conditions. It is lawmaking, because its character-istic function is not the promulgation of laws but the assertion of legal claims for any decree, and law-preserving, because it is at the disposal of these ends . . . Rather, the 'law' of the police really marks the point at which the state, whether from impotence or because of the immanent connections within any legal system, can no longer guarantee through the legal system the empirical ends that it desires at any price to attain.[9]

The political project of the French year II aimed at a universal justice that still continues to remain a hope: that of equality among men as a reciprocity of liberty, of equality among peoples as a reciprocity of sovereignty.

On 20 September 2001, George W. Bush declared: 'The United States respects the people of Afghanistan – after all, we are currently its largest source of human-itarian aid.' In the images seen on television, the logic of arithmetical reparations for domination is expressed in the use of the whip to control hungry people strug-gling for this so-called humanitarian aid.

The violence exercised on 11 September 2001 aimed neither at equality nor liberty. Nor did the preventive war announced by the president of the United States.

---

9   Ibid., p. 243.

Printed in the United States
by Baker & Taylor Publisher Services